MODERN WORLD NATIONS

AFGHANISTAN	IRELAND
ARGENTINA	ISRAEL
AUSTRALIA	ITALY
AUSTRIA	JAMAICA
BAHRAIN	JAPAN
BERMUDA	KAZAKHSTAN
BOLIVIA	KENYA
BOSNIA AND HERZEGOVINA	KUWAIT
BRAZIL	MEXICO
CANADA	THE NETHERLANDS
CHILE	NEW ZEALAND
CHINA	NIGERIA
COSTA RICA	NORTH KOREA
CROATIA	NORWAY
CUBA	PAKISTAN
EGYPT	PERU
ENGLAND	THE PHILIPPINES
ETHIOPIA	RUSSIA
FRANCE	SAUDI ARABIA
REPUBLIC OF GEORGIA	SCOTLAND
GERMANY	SENEGAL
GHANA	SOUTH AFRICA
GUATEMALA	SOUTH KOREA
ICELAND	TAIWAN
INDIA	TURKEY
INDONESIA	UKRAINE
IRAN	UZBEKISTAN
IRAQ	

Peru

Charles F. Gritzner

and

Yvonne Gritzner

Series Consulting Editor
Charles F. Gritzner
South Dakota State University

CHELSEA HOUSE
PUBLISHERS
A Haights Cross Communications Company

Philadelphia

Frontispiece: Flag of Peru

Cover: Perched above the Andean city of Cuzco, Sacsahuacan was the site of a bloody battle in 1536 between the Spaniards and the Incas. It is not known when or how the fortress was built as the stones weigh many tons and the Incas did not use wheeled vehicles.

CHELSEA HOUSE PUBLISHERS

VP, New Product Development Sally Cheney
Director of Production Kim Shinners
Creative Manager Takeshi Takahashi
Manufacturing Manager Diann Grasse

Staff for PERU

Executive Editor Lee Marcott
Production Editor Noelle Nardone
Series Designer Takeshi Takahashi
Cover Designer Keith Trego
Layout 21st Century Publishing and Communications, Inc.
Photo Researcher 21st Century Publishing and Communications, Inc.

A Haights Cross Communications Company

http://www.chelseahouse.com

First Printing

1 3 5 7 9 8 6 4 2

Library of Congress Cataloging-in-Publication Data

Gritzner, Charles F.
   Peru/Charles F. Gritzner, Yvonne Gritzner.
      p. cm.—(Modern world nations)
Includes bibliographical references and index.
   ISBN 0-7910-7478-1
   1. Peru—Juvenile literature. I. Gritzner, Yvonne. II. Title. III. Series.
F3408.5.G75 2004
985—dc22

2004013707

All links and web addresses were checked and verified to be correct at the time of publication. Because of the dynamic nature of the web, some addresses and links may have changed since publication and may no longer be valid.

Table of Contents

1   Introducing Peru   8

2   Land of Environmental Diversity   14

3   Native Cultures   34

4   People and Culture   50

5   Political History and Government   62

6   Peru's Economy: Problems
    and Prospects   74

7   Living in Peru Today   86

8   Peru Looks Ahead   98

    Facts at a Glance   104
    History at a Glance   108
    Further Reading   110
    Index   111

Peru

Introducing Peru

By almost any measure, Peru is one of the world's most fascinating countries. It is also a very troubled land. Few countries have greater potential than does this South American nation; nonetheless, today, Peru looks back on a glorious, yet often turbulent, past and warily looks ahead to an uncertain future. Because of its natural and cultural diversity and many associated problems, the country seems to be locked in an endless cycle of frustration.

In this book, you will come to appreciate why Peru is unique among modern world nations. You will visit its varied and often extreme landscapes, meet its people, and travel through its diverse regions.

The word "spectacular" describes many aspects of Peru—spectacular mountains, spectacular desert landscapes, and spectacular rain forests. It shares the dark blue waters of the world's highest navigable water body, the beautiful Lake Titicaca, with neighboring Bolivia and also can boast of its many historical sites. The

The extinct Nevado Huascaran volcano stands at 22,204 feet (6,768 meters). It is the highest peak in Peru and one of the highest in the Andes. Avalanches in 1962 and 1970 swept down its slopes burying whole towns and villages and killing many thousands of people.

magnificent ruins of Machu Picchu or the ancient and mysterious Nazca Lines have lured thousands of visitors. Peru also is home to 10 World Heritage Sites, a number surpassed in South America only by Brazil.

LAND OF DIVERSITY

No country in the world exceeds Peru in terms of environmental extremes. Within an area of roughly half a million square miles (1.3 million square kilometers) in area, Peru's natural diversity ranges from parched coastal desert to sweltering tropical rain forest. Between these two extreme environments, the towering Andes soar to snow-covered, glacier-scoured peaks whose height is topped only by Asia's Himalayas. Coastal Peru gazes westward across the seemingly endless expanse of the world's largest natural feature, the Pacific Ocean. Only 100 miles (160 kilometers) inland, on the eastern slopes of the Andes, rise the headwaters of the world's greatest river, the Amazon, which flows eastward to the Atlantic.

Because of its varied natural environments, Peru suffers from many natural hazards. The country has suffered a heavy toll from devastating earthquakes, catastrophic landslides, and torrential flooding. Coastal tsunamis (tidal waves), occasional volcanic eruptions, and tropical diseases also pose constant threats to life and also to property. Off Peru's shores, periodic outbursts of El Niño events (described in Chapter 2) have a profound affect on both local and global weather conditions.

Peru's cultural history is as diverse and fascinating as the country's natural landscapes. Early cultures developed what became one of the world's great centers of plant and animal domestication, the basis for all great early civilizations. The "Irish" (white) potato, first cultivated by native peoples of the region, was one of Peru's great gifts to the world. With a reliable diet made possible by the potato and other cultivated crops and the llama as a beast of burden, culture advanced rapidly.

Many different tribal groups advanced in what is now Peru, but none matched the marvelous achievements of the Quechua- and Aymara-speaking peoples popularly known as the Inca. Their level of cultural achievement was, in many ways, unequaled anywhere in the world at the time. In the early sixteenth century, strangers from a distant land arrived on Peru's shores. A handful of Spanish conquistadors under the leadership of Francisco Pizarro toppled the vast, powerful Inca Empire. The country and its culture were forever changed.

In 1535, conquering Spaniards established the city of Lima a few miles inland from the Pacific, in the shadow of the Andes. Lima rapidly rose to prominence as the leading political, economic, cultural, and population center in the emerging Spanish empire on the South American continent. This European city stood in marked contrast to the ancient Inca center of

Cuzco (Cusco), located high in the Andes. Today, nearly five centuries later, these quite different cities serve as symbols—urban reminders of Peru's proud, yet often troubled, history. They also stand as monuments to the striking differences that continue to separate native peoples and their way of life from the conquering Spaniards in this culturally diverse land.

Even today, Spaniards account for only about 15 percent of Peru's estimated 28 to 29 million people. Approximately 8 of every 10 Peruvians are of pure or partial Indian heritage. Since their conquest, however, Spaniards have dominated the country's political, social, and economic institutions. Such an imbalance of power and opportunity is the source of great resentment and tension. Faced with grinding poverty, many farmers have turned to growing coca, the source of the narcotic cocaine. The drug trade has brought wealth to some, but trouble to many. During recent decades, these and other troubles have spawned violent terrorist activity and considerable political instability. Such problems have a negative impact on the country's economy, compounding the frustrations shared by all Peruvians.

PERU'S PLACE IN THE WORLD

All geographic study begins with the question "Where?" Location and its importance are the key to geographic understanding. By knowing where places are, the geographer can put together the pieces of a scientific puzzle that reveals what those places are like. Peru, for example, lies between the equator (0 degrees latitude) and 18 degrees south latitude. This places the country entirely in the Southern Hemisphere and also in the tropical latitudes. For reasons explained in Chapter 2, however, only the country's eastern half experiences conditions usually associated with the "tropics." Peru's Talara peninsula, located in the far northwestern corner of the country, is South America's westernmost spot. Its position, 81 degrees west longitude, places the spot due south of Miami, Florida, and Pittsburgh, Pennsylvania. Only a small portion of North

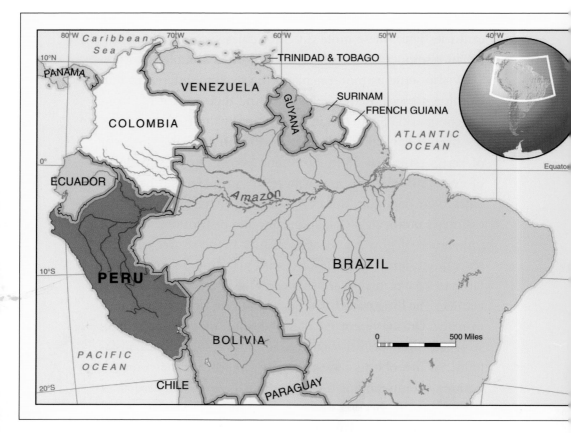

Peru lies between the equator at 0 degrees latitude and 18 degrees south latitude. It is located entirely in the Southern Hemisphere and within the tropical latitudes.

America, therefore, lies directly north of the South American continent. As you will learn in subsequent chapters, this element of location has been quite important to Peru.

Peru is one of 20 Latin-American republics. This sprawling culture region extends from the U.S. border with Mexico southward to the tip of South America. Some Latin-American countries, including Peru, retain many Indian customs. Throughout the region, however, language, religion, customs, and other aspects of culture have Latin roots in Europe's Iberian Peninsula (Spain and, in the case of Brazil, Portugal).

Economically, Peru falls within the Pacific Rim. This region includes all countries facing the Pacific Ocean, including the United States, Japan, Canada, China, and Mexico, and is now the focal point of about three-quarters of all world trade.

Narrowing the focus somewhat, geographers often refer to Peru as a central Andean country. It shares this regional identity with its northern neighbor, Ecuador, and southeastern neighbor, Bolivia. To the south, the country shares a short border with Chile. To the northeast and east, in the remote, vast, and thinly populated tropical lowlands, Peru shares boundaries with Colombia and Brazil.

A CYCLE OF FRUSTRATION

As is true of most, if not all, less-developed countries (LDCs), Peru is locked in a seemingly never-ending "cycle of frustration." This concept, developed some years ago by the author, can help us better understand the tremendous complexity of the many problems that affect countries such as Peru. In essence, the cycle addresses the ways in which eight geographic categories affect one another in a seemingly never-ending cycle, leading to social, economic, and political frustration. The factors are native cultural heritage, European cultural heritage, natural environment and resource base, economic system and conditions, infrastructure, settlement patterns and trends, demographic (population) conditions and trends, and political institutions and government. Each factor influences and is influenced in turn by the others. The cycle of frustration is an integrating theme that is considered in the context of each chapter.

In the next chapter, you will study Peru's natural landscapes as you visit its coastal deserts, the Andean highlands, and eastern tropical lowlands. You will also be introduced to the country's natural hazards and other environmental problems. Of greatest importance, you will better understand the tremendous economic potential that is offered by the country's varied and scenic natural landscapes.

2

Land of Environmental Diversity

"Spectacular" and "diverse" are two words often used in reference to Peru's natural environment. In terms of its landform features, climates and ecosystems, water features, animal life, soils, and other natural conditions, perhaps no other country can match the extremes found in Peru. The coastal Peruvian Desert, which reaches southward into Chile as the Atacama (the same desert with a different name), is the world's driest. Just miles inland, the high Andean crests, plateaus, and valleys rise to snow-covered heights and then within just a few miles plunge into the steaming tropical rain forests of the upper Amazon basin. On a micro scale, where else in the world would it be possible to stand in one spot and see tropical rain forest, snow-capped peaks, cacti and desert scrub, and mid-latitude woodlands and grasslands within a radius of several miles? Such diversity is made possible only by great changes in elevation.

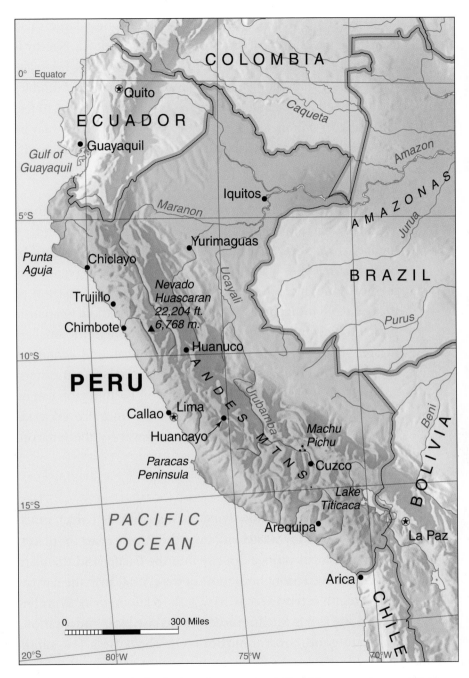

Peru's wide range of physical environments, defined by ruggedness, extreme aridity, and wetness in its various locales, has produced a country with a scattered population and relatively poor agricultural performance.

Peru shares with Bolivia the world's highest large (also navigable to steamships!) body of water, Lake Titicaca. Nearby is the world's deepest canyon. The mighty Amazon River begins its 4,000-mile (6,440-kilometer) journey to the sea where it tumbles from Lake McIntyre, hidden away at an elevation of 17,220 feet (5,250 meters) in the southern Andes. Welcome to what may be the world's most spectacular and diverse natural wonderland!

LAND FEATURES

Peru's land features generally fall within one of three regions: a narrow coastal plain (*la costa*), the central Andean highlands (*la sierra*), and the vast Amazon basin (*la selva*). In human terms, the rugged central Andean highlands region was the heartland of the Inca Empire. Today, it is home to most of the country's indigenous (native Indian) population. Spaniards settled mainly in the coastal zone, which, although the smallest in area, is the country's population, political, and economic heart. The mountains served as a huge barrier between eastern and western Peru. Even today, the Amazon Basin region can be reached only by air and a small number of unimproved roads leading to rivers—rivers are the main highways of the Amazon. Few people inhabit this remote area.

Coastal Plain

A narrow band of low-lying coastal plain (la costa), much of which is a sandy wasteland, hugs the Pacific coast. In places, mountain slopes plunge directly into the Pacific and the plain is nonexistent. Throughout most of the coastal strip the narrow plain's width rarely exceeds 10 miles (16 kilometers). With few exceptions (such as Chimbote), the coast lacks indentations to create good natural harbors. Off shore lie a few small, scattered islands.

For reasons explained elsewhere in this chapter, the coastal plain generally is extremely dry. In some places, however, streams beginning high in the Andes flow across this forbidding coastal zone to the Pacific. Approximately 40 small streams carry enough water to create an oasis. Such areas attract crop production and settlement. From the air, the Peruvian coast appears as a barren north–south strip crossed in places by thin bands of green with a community located near the sea. Because of their rapid velocity as they descend from high elevations toward sea level, the streams carry a heavy load of sand and silt (soil with rock particles). When deposited, this material is rapidly picked up and shifted by winds, creating the vast expanses of sand dunes that cover much of the coastal plain. Dunes may reach a height of 200 feet (60 meters). Some are active: They are constantly shifting and thus pose a threat to settlements, transportation routes, and oasis agricultural lands.

Andean Highlands

The Andean highlands (recognized locally as la sierra) are the "gift" of two tectonic plates—two huge masses of Earth's crust that are "floating" and moving. Along most of South America's western margin, the South American Plate (the huge chunk of Earth's surface that forms the continent) and Nazca Plate (within the eastern Pacific basin) are colliding. These two huge masses of earth are colliding at a combined speed of slightly more than three inches (eight centimeters) per year—a tremendous velocity when measured by geologic time!

Because of the geological instability along the margin of tectonic plates, several things happen in the zone of impact. Acting as a giant bulldozer, the Nazca Plate piles land high in the form of the Andes Mountains. Earth movements also contribute to seismic instability, resulting in frequent and often devastating earthquakes. With pressure released by giant fissures (cracks in Earth's crust along the edges of the plates), molten material can work its way to the surface and form volcanoes.

The Andes form the longest and second-highest mountain range in the world. In Peru, more than 30 peaks rise above 19,000 feet (5,790 meters). The country's tallest, Nevado Huascaran, soars to a height of 22,205 feet (6,768 meters), making it the fourth-highest mountain in the Western Hemisphere. This is only 629 feet (192 meters)—about twice the length of a football field—shorter than Mount Aconcagua (between Chile and Argentina), the highest peak in the Western Hemisphere!

Many of the country's mountains that reach above 16,000 feet (5,000 meters) have been, and continue to be, heavily glaciated, even though they are located in the tropical latitudes. Glaciers have created spectacularly jagged features, contributing to the scenic beauty of the highlands.

The land changes south of Lima. Here, and continuing into Bolivia, a number of volcanic peaks rise above adjacent high plateau surfaces formed by lava flows. El Misti, which rises to an elevation of 19,100 feet (5,822 meters) above the city of Arequipa, is the country's highest and best-known volcano. A small portion of the Bolivian Altiplano, a high intermontane plateau, extends into southern Peru in the area of Lake Titicaca.

Southwestern Peru is home to three of the world's deepest canyons: Colca, Cotahuasi, and Apurimac. Apurimac Canyon, located between Apurimac and Cuzco, was recently measured at 15,656 feet (4,772 meters) deep, or three times deeper than the Grand Canyon, making it the world's deepest gorge by a considerable margin. Colca, located near Arequipa, is the best known of the three canyons, no doubt because it is the most accessible to tourists. This spectacular gorge, with walls terraced in many places by ancient farming peoples and a depth of 10,500 feet (3,200 meters), is twice as deep as the Grand Canyon. Until recently, it was believed to be the world's deepest. Tourists also flock to Colca to see the canyon's condors, which, with a 10-foot (3-meter) wingspan, are the world's largest birds. Each morning, hundreds of condors leave their nests. Using updrafts created by early morning breezes, these magnificent birds begin aerobatic maneuvers described as one of South America's most impressive sights.

The Andean crest forms the South American continental divide, the ridge separating the headwaters of streams that flow westward to the Pacific or eastward to the Atlantic. Because of more humid conditions resulting in greatly increased erosion, the eastern slope of the Andes has been carved into numerous deep, narrow valleys. Steep, heavily eroded terrain makes construction of transportation routes both difficult and costly. As a result, there are few surface linkages joining coastal and highland Peru to the eastern Andean foothills and beyond across the vast eastern lowland.

Eastern Plains of the Amazon Basin

Approximately half of Peru lies east of the Andes, on the vast plain of the Amazon basin, which extends 2,000 miles (3,220 kilometers) eastward to the Atlantic Ocean. Near the Andean foothills, where the plain rises to meet the mountains, streams have carved a more rugged landscape known locally as the *montaña*. Eastward, elevations drop rapidly and the land flattens out. Peruvians call the region la selva (meaning "the rain forest"). In many places, the huge structural basin across which the Amazon River and its tributaries flow has been filled to a depth of thousands of feet by alluvium—stream-deposited sediments carried from the Andes. Such soils offer some agricultural potential, but the region suffers from isolation and minimal economic development.

WEATHER AND CLIMATE

Similar to Peru's landform regions, the country is also divided into three major zones of weather and climate. The country's atmospheric conditions are affected by three primary controls: a cold coastal ocean current, Peru's location within the tropical latitudes, and elevation. Peru is the only country that can boast of having some of the worlds most parched desert landscapes, snow- and glacier-capped mountain peaks, *and* vast expanses of tropical rain forest.

Weather is the day-to-day condition of the atmosphere. Its conditions include temperature, precipitation (rain, snow, hail, or sleet), atmospheric pressure, and wind. A fifth category, storms, results from extremes in one or more of the listed conditions.

Climate is the long-term average of weather conditions. Generally speaking, Peru's climate has a great range in precipitation from place to place, but does not suffer from high or low temperature extremes. Winds tend to be reliable, and the country does not experience severe tropical storms such as hurricanes or typhoons, although El Niño events do cause occasional catastrophic weather disruptions in the form of rains on the coastal desert that cause flooding and mudslides.

Temperature

Temperatures throughout most of Peru can best be described as "mild" and "monotonous" (unchanging). Places located within the tropical latitudes generally experience very consistent temperatures, with little daily or seasonal variation. Regardless of the season, the sun is never far from overhead during its daily passage. Other major factors influencing the country's temperatures are the cold waters of the Peru Current and elevation.

Deserts usually are places of extreme heat. This is not the case in Peru. Waters of the cold Peru Current keep temperatures of the low-lying narrow coastal region quite low. Record high temperatures for Tumbes and Lima, for example, are in the low 90s F (30s C) even though the cities lie only 4 and 12 degrees, respectively, south of the equator! Along the desert coast, lowest temperatures range from the mid-50s F (12° to 13° C) in the north to the mid-30s F (1.5° C) in the far south. The record low in Lima is a comfortable 45° F (7° C).

In the highlands, temperatures vary with elevation. As a general rule, temperature drops approximately 3.5° F (1° C) with each 1,000-foot (300-meter) increase in elevation. Cuzco, located at about 11,000 feet (3,350 meters) above sea level, experiences occasional freezing temperatures during the winter months, with record lows falling into the mid-teens F (-9.5° C). Highest temperatures in Cuzco, on the other hand, rarely reach into the low

80s F (27° to 28° C). The snow line, or elevation above which temperatures average below freezing, is approximately 17,000 to 18,000 feet (5,200 to 5,500 meters). Higher peaks are locked into a permanent polar chill and, even though they are in the tropical latitudes, they have permanent blankets of snow and glacial ice.

Roughly half of Peru lies in the upper Amazon basin—the world's largest tropical lowland. Here, temperatures are extremely monotonous, varying little from day to day or season to season. Iquitos, the largest city in eastern Peru, is located 3 degrees south of the equator. Its range in temperatures is typical of the region: Coolest to warmest monthly averages range only 3 degrees, from 78° to 81° F (25.5° to 27.2° C). The lowest record temperatures are in the mid-50s F (12° to 13° C), and the highest for most of the region rarely reach 100° F (38° C). The author was in Iquitos on the day it experienced its record low temperature of 54° F (12.2° C). He was traveling with a group of teachers from Alaska who thought the break from sweltering tropical conditions was wonderful. Local people, however, did not share that enthusiasm. They were shivering and quite miserable!

Precipitation

Precipitation (rain, snow, hail, sleet) in Peru varies greatly. Under normal (non–El Niño) conditions, the desert coast receives only a few inches of moisture and a year or more may pass with no rainfall whatsoever in some of the drier locations. Lima normally receives less than 2 inches (50 millimeters) of rain per year.

Several factors combine to create the coastal aridity. Of greatest importance is the presence of the cold Peru Current just off the coast. As moisture-bearing air from the Pacific Ocean passes across the current and over the coastal region, it warms. Warming air increases its moisture-holding capacity rather than giving up its moisture as rain. Occasionally, warm water replaces the Peru Current in an event called El Niño.

Half of Peru lies in the upper Amazon basin—the world's largest tropical lowland. Hundreds of streams flow from the Andes into its tributaries and because of this dense network of rivers many people and goods travel by water.

When this occurs, heavy rains can fall, causing widespread flooding and destruction in the coastal desert region.

To the east, in the humid tropical part of the country, rain falls almost daily in what can be torrential convectional storms (thundershowers). Much of the region receives about 80 inches (2,000 millimeters) of rain per year, with some locations receiving even more. Iquitos, for example, averages 104 inches (2,640 millimeters). As in most climatic regions, the high sun period here is the rainy period of the year. In the tropical latitudes, though, the sun passes overhead twice each year—at Peru's latitude, during the spring and fall months, making them the wettest.

Precipitation amounts vary greatly in the mountains. Generally, the eastern slopes of the Andes are much wetter than those facing westward, which are quite dry. At higher elevations, snow can fall during any month of the year. Cuzco receives about 30 inches (760 millimeters) of precipitation per year, sometimes in the form of snow.

El Niño

During recent decades, people throughout the world have become increasingly aware of what appears to be a very important "trigger" of major short-term weather change: the El Niño phenomenon. El Niño (named for the Christ child because of its tendency to appear during the Christmas season) appears to be responsible for wide-ranging conditions of drought or flood, higher or lower temperatures, increasing storm frequency, and other weather problems in many parts of the world. In essence, El Niño is a condition in which the cold water of the Peru Current off the coast of Peru and Ecuador is replaced by warm water of the tropical Pacific. The mechanics of why this happens are not yet fully understood. El Niño, however, appears to be yet another of Peru's contributions to the world! In Peru, its primary effect is to bring heavy rains and much warmer temperatures to the coastal desert region.

Coastal Fog

A visitor to Lima or elsewhere along the Peruvian coast during the winter months will be amazed that the sky can be so overcast and the humidity so high (often 100 percent) yet very little rain falls and the land is bone dry, gray, and nearly lifeless desert! This is *garúa* (*garrua*), the dense Peruvian fog that hugs the coastal region during the winter months of June, July, and August. By definition, fog is a cloud that is at ground level. Here, as on the Southern California coast, which experiences a similar phenomenon, the garúa appears as a low bank of dense stratus clouds, or fog. Only when viewing the garúa from above does one realize that the layer is very shallow, less than 3,000 feet (915 meters), and that it barely reaches into the nearby mountain foothills. During the winter months, many coastal people enjoy going to the mountains, where the sun is almost always shining.

PLANT AND ANIMAL LIFE

Weather and climate are the key contributors to a region's ecosystems—its plant and animal life. Peru therefore can be divided into three zones: desert, mountain, and tropical rain forest. Also of great importance to Peru is its abundant marine life. Few places on earth support as great a diversity of ecosystems.

Desert

Along the immediate coast and on slopes of adjacent foothills, the garúa creates a fog zone, or *loma* (meaning "low hill"), that supports limited plant life. About 1,000 species of hardy ferns, flowering plants, and other flora have been identified in this zone. These plants play a role in sustaining their own lives! Moisture in the fog forms dew on the plants. The dew drips down the plant and to the ground, providing necessary moisture. Because of the aridity, few large animals inhabit the coastal region. Loma meadows do support a few small animals, as well as a variety of birds and insects.

Mountain

Mountain ecosystems vary with latitude, elevation, and exposure to the prevailing sunlight. The Central Andes are no exception. In fact, it was in the Andes that German geographer Alexander von Humboldt first recognized the significance of vertical zonation. Almost 200 years ago, he created the basic model that is still used in many textbooks today, showing changes in natural vegetation and land use patterns at various elevations.

At lower elevations, the Peruvian Andes have arid conditions and a desert ecosystem on their western flank and the humid tropical rain forest (montaña) along the lower eastern slopes. At high elevations, the mountains have arctic conditions

Llamas are domesticated animals in Peru and herds of these animals grazing have become a defining image of the Peruvian highlands.

of snow and ice and no plant and animal life. Among these three extremes, nearly all of Earth's intermediate ecosystems can be found. Western slopes support dryland scrub (stunted tree or shrub) species in places and dense forest cover in others. Brush and "mountain forest," a dense growth of trees smaller than those of the rain forest, extend up the eastern slope to an elevation of about 11,000 feet (3,350 meters). Above this elevation and extending to the lifeless mountain peaks, trees give way to various communities of shrubs and mountain grasslands called *puna*. These grassy plains and hills extend for hundreds of miles through Peru's highlands. Ichu grass dominates this ecosystem. It grows in scattered tussocks (tufts) often a foot (.3 meter) thick and up to 3 feet (1 meter) high. The puna is home to domesticated llamas and alpacas and wild vicuñas. One of the most defining images of the Peruvian highlands is herds of these animals grazing on ichu grass.

Rain Forest

As the eastern slopes of the Andes give way to the lowland plains, the upland flora gives way to tropical rain forest (selva), the world's most diverse ecosystem. Because of its isolation and various environmental limitations, however, this is Peru's least-populated and most poorly developed region. Abundant moisture and constantly high temperatures combine to create an environmental hothouse in which both plant and animal life thrive. Millions of floral and faunal species make their home in the rain forest.

Dozens of different tree species compete with one another as their crowns struggle toward sunlight at heights occasionally reaching up to 200 feet (60 meters). The crowns create an overhead canopy that prevents sunlight from reaching the forest floor. In this eerie, dark-green, shaded environment, few plants can grow. Unlike images of "jungle" produced by Hollywood, the forest floor is relatively clear. The trees, tangled vines, and other plant life that make an all but impenetrable jungle grow only where sunlight can reach the forest floor. True jungle is found only along streams, roadways, agricultural fields, or other cleared areas.

In the rain forest, each tree can be host to literally millions of smaller plants—mosses, lichens, bromeliads, vines, and many other species. Some species have flaring buttresses at their base, a condition some scientists believe to be an adaptation to the region's very high water table.

The rain forest habitat supports very few large animals. Monkeys, the strange-looking tapir, leopards, and various rodents are the largest land animals. Insects and birds abound, and snakes, including many deadly varieties, are plentiful. When visiting for the first time, a visitor is bound to be awed (and perhaps frightened!) by the strange sounds made by nature's rain forest orchestra. The tropical waters teem with fish and other fauna, some of which—such as the piranha, electric eel, and huge boa constrictor—are potentially deadly.

Marine

The marine ecosystem has always played a very important role in Peru's economy. Early peoples turned to the sea for food and other resources. During recent decades, Peru has ranked among the world's leaders in its harvest of marine resources. You have already learned how the cold waters of the Peru Current contribute to the extreme aridity and dense seasonal fog of the coastal zone. You have seen how conditions can abruptly change—with cold water replaced by the warm waters of an El Niño event, bringing rain, flooding, and higher temperatures.

Geographers, perhaps more than any other scientists, emphasize the study of interrelationships or interactions as they attempt to explain conditions. Coastal Peru offers a wonderful case study of the geographic way of studying a place and its features: guano.

Guano is bird droppings. That, though, is just the beginning of the story. Along the central part of South America's Pacific coast, prevailing winds blow the ocean's surface water westward toward Asia. In order to maintain sea level, this water is replaced by an upwelling (rising) of nutrient-rich cold water from the ocean floor. Trillions of tiny plankton (small marine organisms) thrive in the cold waters immediately off the coast. Plankton, in turn, is the food supply for billions of fish, including huge schools of small anchovies. The anchovies? They are the primary food source for millions of seabirds—cormorants, pelicans, boobies, and others—that are attracted to the area to feast on the marine abundance.

With millions of birds, however, millions of tons of bird droppings accumulate through time on a small number of "Guano Islands" that dot the Peruvian coast. The islands are often little more than barren specks of rock rising above the water. Over thousands of years, in the nearly rainless environment, the guano accumulated in huge deposits, often tens of feet deep in places.

Centuries ago, Indians in the region began using the guano as fertilizer. They were the only native people in the Americas to deliberately fertilize crops. (The theory that northeast Woodland tribes in what is now the United States fertilized hills of corn with fish has been proven to be a myth.) Soon, the nitrogen-rich guano began to be exported to Europe and North America. As you might imagine, mining conditions were horrible, and the Spaniards introduced Chinese laborers to work the guano deposits. (Today, about 1 percent of the country's population can trace its ancestry to these workers). Increased production for export resulted in serious overmining, which, in turn, caused severe damage to the marine bird habitat and nests, resulting in a sharp decline in production. Today, this once-important resource has all but been replaced by synthetic fertilizers.

WATER FEATURES

Water features create three of Peru's "windows to the world": the Pacific Ocean, which provides a link to all countries bordering the Pacific Rim; Lake Titicaca, which opens onto adjoining Bolivia; and the upper Amazon River drainage system, which provides a very distant link through Brazil to the Atlantic basin and beyond.

The importance of the Pacific Ocean, with particular emphasis on the Peru Current and the periodic El Niño events, has been discussed elsewhere in this chapter, as has the ocean's role in the context of guano. Economic aspects of the Pacific will be discussed in their appropriate context.

Lake Titicaca is one of the world's most spectacular natural features. Its elevation, at 12,500 feet (3,810 meters), its size, and its deep blue waters and the area's unique history and culture make it a popular tourist destination. The lake occupies an area of about 3,250 square miles (8,400 square kilometers), making

Lake Titicaca, divided between Peru and Bolivia, is the largest enclosed body of water in South America. Fishing boats, called *balsas*, have been made by the Uru Indians for many years and can still be seen on the lake's waters. These reed boats are made of bundled cattail reeds.

it the largest enclosed water body in South America. It fills a small portion of the Altiplano, the huge mountain basin that extends northward from Bolivia into southern Peru. Because the lake has only one small outward-flowing river, its water is slightly brackish (salty) and contains only a few species of fish. Titicaca is also a very deep lake, reaching a depth of 920 feet (280 meters) and averaging 460 to 600 feet (140 to 180 meters).

In dimensions, the lake reaches 122 miles (196 kilometers) long at its greatest northwest–southeast extent and averages about 35 miles (56 kilometers) in width. Despite the mountains surrounding it, there are points at which one can gaze across the lake and not see land on the distant horizon.

At an elevation of nearly two and a half miles (four kilometers) above sea level, Titicaca is the world's highest navigable water body. Yes, steamboats ply its waters! The first such craft, which began operation in 1862, was built in England and carried to the lake piece by piece on mules. Today, the lake can be crossed in a matter of hours by modern hydrofoil craft. Titicaca's most famous craft, however, are the balsas, or reed boats, made by Uru Indians. The canoelike craft are made from dried bundles of totora (cattail) reeds that are bound together.

East of the continental divide, all Peruvian rivers ultimately flow into the Amazon drainage system, which in Peru is recognized by a local name, the Marañón. Although there is controversy concerning the precise location of the Amazon's headwaters, all contenders are located in southern Peru. There, from the high Andean peaks, small streams flow into the Apurimac and Urubamba rivers, which, in turn, join to become the Ucayali River. The Ucayali then joins the Marañón. Hundreds of streams flow from the Andes into these and other tributaries. Because of the dense network of rivers, land routes are all but nonexistent in eastern Peru; travel is by water or air. On its 4,000-mile (6,437-kilometer) journey to the Atlantic, the Amazon is navigable by ocean-going ships from the port city of Iquitos to its mouth, a distance of 1,900 miles (3,060 kilometers).

NATURAL HAZARDS

Perhaps to a greater extent than any other Latin-American country, Peru is subject to a variety of natural hazards. In fact, the country was the site of the worst natural disaster in the history of the Western Hemisphere. In 1970, an earthquake measuring 7.7 on the Richter scale shook loose a huge

The winding Urubamba River runs down the heavily forested eastern slopes of the Andes mountains. From these high Andean peaks small streams flow into the Urubamba River and join to become the Ucayali River.

block of ice and rock that catapulted into the valleys below. The provincial capital of Yungay and more than a dozen other communities were buried under a blanket of stone and mud debris. When the final toll was taken, an estimated 69,000 people were dead, another 140,000 injured, and more than 500,000 were left homeless.

Because of its location on the edge of two tectonic plates, Peru is subject to extensive seismic (earthquake) activity. Each year, the country experiences as many as 200 tremors. Since the mid-1500s, the country has been rocked by more than 70 violent quakes, an average of one every seven to eight years. In addition to direct destruction, earthquakes also trigger avalanches and tsunamis, both of which cause widespread death and devastation in Peru. In 2001, an earthquake with a magnitude of 8.4 struck near Peru's southern coast, affecting the Arequipa-Tacna-Camana area. An estimated 75 people died, many more were injured, and nearly 50,000 buildings were destroyed or damaged. Landslides buried many highways in the region. At the coastal city of Camana, the resulting tsunami struck as a series of four waves that surged inland with water as deep as 26 feet (8 meters). The resulting flood reached inland for up to three-quarters of a mile (1.2 kilometers), killing nearly 140 people and destroying thousands of buildings.

In the parched coastal deserts of Peru's coastal zone, periodic floods triggered by El Niño events are a major environmental hazard. In the dry landscape, even small amounts of rain can cause severe flash flooding and mudslides. In the eastern tropical lowlands, tropical diseases pose a hazard, as do venomous and constricting snakes, disease-bearing insects, and a variety of aquatic life, including the piranha fish.

Most Peruvians live on the edge in terms of potential environmental threats. Those living along the Pacific coast know that earthquakes frequently rock their area. Death and destruction can come from the sea in the form of a huge tsunami or from the mountains with El Niño-induced flash floods. Inland, seismic events, landslides, and avalanches pose a constant threat. The city of Huaraz, home to 60,000 people, lives in constant fear of yet another environmental hazard. Lake Palcacocha sits in a valley above the city, but above the lake is a huge glacier that has developed a large fissure. If a large piece of the glacier breaks off and falls into the lake, the resulting flood would reach—and inundate—the city in about 12 minutes. In 1941, nearly 7,000 people in the city were killed by a similar event.

NATURAL ENVIRONMENT AND THE CYCLE OF FRUSTRATION

Nature has contributed to Peru's cycle of frustration in many ways. First, it has divided the country into three separate zones—the dry west, the rugged interior, and the remote eastern tropical lowlands. Second, it has contributed to a division of the country's people by race, ethnicity, language, and tribal affiliation—the Spanish influence dominates the coastal zone, Quechua/Inca culture and heritage do so in the highlands, and a number of Amazon Indian groups in the east. Third, because of the difficulty and cost of building transportation link-ages in mountain and rainforest environments, settlement and economic development lag in perhaps two-thirds of the country. Fourth, a variety of natural hazards have taken a costly toll on the peoples' spirits and the country's economy. Finally, because of a combination of these factors, Peru is an extremely difficult country to govern successfully.

3

Native Cultures

P eru's native cultural history is no less spectacular and diverse than its varied natural environments. In the Western Hemisphere, perhaps only Mexico can equal the many accomplishments of its early aboriginal populations. And only Mexico, with the Spanish conquest of the Aztec, experienced a comparable violent clash of cultures. In Peru, a handful of Spaniards conquered the advanced, vast, and powerful Inca Empire. As is true throughout much of Latin America, since the time of conquest, racial and cultural diversity has been the source of socioeconomic stratification and political conflict.

In this chapter, you will learn about the many achievements of Peru's native cultures. You will also learn how a small number of Europeans were able to topple a powerful civilization and impose their own cultural imprint on the land.

THE FIRST PERUVIANS

No one knows much about the origin of the first Peruvians. During the twentieth century, archaeologists (scientists who study early cultures) thought they had answers to most questions relating to the earliest Americans. Now, they are less certain; in fact, the more that is known about early Americans, the less sure we are about who they were, where they came from, how they traveled, or when they arrived. For nearly a century, it was believed that America's earliest people came from northeastern Asia. Their route, according to archaeologists, was by way of Beringia—the Bering Strait "land bridge." During the Ice Age, sea level dropped perhaps 350 to 400 feet (107 to 122 meters), exposing much of what is now the Bering Strait. This dry land supposedly made it possible for big game hunters to cross from Siberia to Alaska. An ice-free corridor between two huge North American ice sheets is believed to have created a pathway southward into what is now Canada. From there, these hunters spread rapidly through the Americas. The people were Mongoloid (the primary race of people living in eastern Asia). They supposedly arrived 12,000 to 20,000 years ago.

During recent years, some archaeologists, geographers, and others have challenged many of these beliefs. They doubt that people could have survived the cold temperatures of a land crossing between two glaciers. In fact, some doubt that an ice-free corridor ever existed! Might the early migrants have followed a much warmer coastal route on land and along the glaciers' edge by water? Some scientists now believe that such a route might have been followed. In fact, a coastal route appeared on the October 2000 *National Geographic Magazine* map supplement, "Peopling of the Americas." There is also increasing evidence that early humans reached southern South America more than 30,000 years ago. This compounds the mystery surrounding the first Americans, because it is nearly twice as long as indicated by accepted evidence of human presence in North America!

Geographically, it is not important to know who the first Peruvians were or when, how, or from where they arrived. We can assume that they were hunting and gathering peoples who had meager possessions and left little lasting imprint on the land or present-day culture (way of life). They probably were here at least 12,000 years ago and possibly longer. An archaeological site near Ayacucho suggests a human presence in the area dating back 18,000 to 20,000 years. By 10,000 B.P. (Before Present), people were well established both in the Andean highlands and in valley oases along the Pacific coast. In the highlands, small groups lived by hunting (the then-wild) llama, alpaca, vicuña, guanaco, and deer—animals that grazed on the grasslands of the puna. They lived a nomadic life, moving up and down valleys to take advantage of plants and animals as they became available during different seasons of the year. Along the coast, populations were somewhat larger and the people were more sedentary. They were able to provide quite well for themselves from the narrow coastal valleys. Resources were abundant both from the sea (fish, shellfish, crustaceans, and seaweed) and land (eggs of marine birds, plant seeds and roots).

Early people also occupied the Amazon basin. Because of the hot tropical conditions, little record exists of their presence in Peru's eastern lowlands.

STEPS TOWARD CIVILIZATION

A productive system of agriculture appears to have been the key to the development of all early civilizations. The transition from food collecting to food production marked one of humankind's biggest leaps forward in terms of cultural development. In this context, culture is defined as a people's way of life—their knowledge and material goods, beliefs and traditions, tools and skills, language and religion, social interactions, and so forth.

Many early civilizations, including those in Peru, depended on irrigation systems. To develop an agricultural system based upon irrigation requires a strong central authority and social organization. There must be a source of power or influence that can direct the work, allocate precious water resources, and both organize and maintain control over society.

Peru was one of the world's earliest and greatest centers of plant and animal domestication and cultivation. There is evidence that crops such as beans and peppers were grown as early as 8500 B.C. Many other crops, including maize (corn), cotton, squash, several varieties of beans, tubers including potatoes and sweet potatoes, and a number of different fruits, came later.

The "Irish," or white, potato, is Peru's primary crop gift to the world. In fact, it is the world's fourth most important agricultural crop and food staple. Potatoes were first cultivated in the central Andes and continue to be the staple crop of highland peoples today. The potato is so important to native Peruvians that the Quechua language has more than 1,000 words for the nutritious tuber. After the conquest, Spaniards carried the potato to Europe, and from Spain, it spread rapidly northward, including to Ireland. During the mid-1800s, the potato crop in Ireland failed, resulting in a famine. Many Irish people moved to the United States, where they introduced their preferred food staple, hence the name "Irish" potato.

Peru also was the New World's primary center of animal domestication. The llama, alpaca, and vicuña were domesticated in the region. The llama, in particular, has played a very important role in Andean life. This animal is highly revered by Amerindians. Its wool is used in making clothing, hide is used for footwear and other items made of leather, the long hair is used for rope, and the animal's meat is a staple, often eaten as *charqui* (dried jerky). Even the dung is dried and used as fuel in home stoves.

In some coastal areas, village life appears to have predated productive crop agriculture by as much as 2,000 years. This could happen only in the presence of an alternative and highly productive food resource base. In this case, it is almost certain that coastal-dwelling peoples turned to the sea and its abundant supply of foodstuffs. In fact, archaeologists have discovered the existence of close links, with accompanying trade, between coastal fishing villages and inland farming communities. By

2000 B.C., settled villages dependent primarily on productive farming appeared both in the highlands and along the coast. In addition to the elaborate irrigation systems, most settlements had pyramids and other ceremonial centers. This provides further evidence of a strong central authority that could provide organizational leadership to a highly stratified society. The stage was set for the emergence and rise of complex societies recognized as early civilizations.

EARLY CIVILIZATIONS

The key to Peruvian civilization may lie nestled in the windswept desert landscape of Peru's Supe Valley. Sandwiched between the Pacific Ocean and the Andes, are the ruins of a city—Caral—that appears to have flourished as early as 3000 B.C. Some archaeologists believe that Caral is the oldest established community in the Americas (and among the most ancient in the world). It is nearly 1,000 years older than sites in Mexico that previously were believed to be the first urban centers in the New World. Caral's six pyramids, other public structures, and residential buildings cover an area of about 150 acres (60 hectares), or one-quarter square mile (.65 square kilometer). Although the city was located 14 miles (22.5 kilometers) inland from the ocean, fish provided the primary source of protein. Crops included sweet potatoes, beans, and squash. Many items found in the ruins came from elsewhere, suggesting that Caral was a thriving center of trade. Where, how, and with whom remain lingering questions, the answers to which may provide valuable clues to the origin of civilization in this region of the world.

Most, if not all, of Peru's coastal oasis sites were settled and densely populated by 1000 B.C. Streams flowing from the Andes provided precious water resources that supported the irrigated farming. Important crops included sweet potatoes, beans, squash, and cotton. Irrigation works were extensive, often diverting water for many miles before distributing it across fields in a series of smaller canals.

Archaeologists from San Marcos University in Lima conduct excavations on ruins at Caral that are believed to be nearly 5,000 years old. Many items found there suggest that it was a thriving center for trade in past millennia.

CULTURES OF THE NORTH COAST

Among the various pre-Incan cultures that developed in the north, the best known are the Moche (also called Mochica) and Chimu. The Moche culture thrived from about 200 to 800 A.D. It occupied a series of 13 river valleys, including that of the Moche River, near present-day Trujillo, and stretched 250 miles (400 kilometers) along the northern coast. In order to survive in this hostile environment, the Moche developed a very elaborate system of irrigation involving diversion dams and weirs (dams that divert or restrict water flow), canals that included aqueducts, and smaller channels to distribute water across fields. The largest canal was about 17 miles (27 kilometers) long. Settlement clustered around massive pyramids. Huaca del Sol (Pyramid of the Sun) was constructed from 100 million adobe bricks and was the largest pre-Columbian structure in South America.

Moche society was very stratified. At the top were priests and warriors. They were followed by middle-class artisans. Moche potters, weavers, metal workers, and others created some of the finest examples of pre-Columbian arts and crafts found in the Americas. A step below were the farmers and fishermen, who provided food and fiber for the population, which may have reached 50,000 people. The Moche fished to provide protein to their diet and also traded. They had sturdy vessels and were skilled navigators. Finally, there was a lower class that included slaves and servants. For unknown reasons—perhaps serious flooding associated with El Niño, pressure from neighboring cultures, or increasing internal social tensions—the Moche culture went into slow decline around A.D. 800.

Along the northern coast, on the ruins of Moche culture, rose the highly organized Chimu Empire, which flourished from about A.D. 1000 to 1470. At its peak, Chimu spread over more than 800 miles (1,290 kilometers) of coastal plain, extending into Ecuador. The capital, Chan Chan, was located just north of present-day Trujillo and may have been the largest city in pre-Columbian South America. At its peak, it had an estimated 50,000 people who occupied 10,000 adobe (earth brick) structures that covered an area of 11 square miles (28.5 square kilometers). The sprawling settlement was divided into a number of self-contained quadrangles, each of which had palaces, temples, homes, markets, storage facilities, and workshops. There were also reservoirs for water storage. Each quadrangle had a pyramid and other ceremonial centers, such as burial mounds. Like other Andean cultures, Chimu society was highly stratified.

As had the Moche, the Chimu specialized in irrigated agriculture, trade, and coastal fishing to provide their needs. In the Chan Chan region, agriculture was fed by a 50-mile-long canal (80.5 kilometers), which eventually grew to an 87-mile-long network (140 kilometers) linking two valleys. Guano was used to fertilize the fields, and cotton was added to the list of crops and valuable trade items. Trade was by both land and water. On land, llama caravans brought goods from the interior Andean highlands.

The extent of Chimu water travel remains somewhat of a mystery. It is known that they had very sturdy craft capable of traveling the high seas and were skilled seamen. Some archaeologists and cultural geographers believe that there is evidence to suggest that they sailed widely. The sweet potato, for example, was a staple crop throughout much of the Pacific basin by the time the first Europeans arrived in the region. It also was called by the same name (*cumar*, in several variations of spelling). Who were the early adventurers who were responsible for its distribution?

Some scholars, including the author, believe that the Hohokam, an early people in Arizona who had a very advanced irrigation technology and many other South American traits, may have originated in Peru. Others, such as archaeologist and adventurer Thor Heyerdahl, saw a strong Peruvian cultural imprint on Easter Island. Heyerdahl believed so strongly in a coastal Peru–Pacific Ocean basin link that he set out to prove that it could have happened. In 1947, he and his crew sailed westward from the Peruvian port city of Callao in a balsa wood raft named *Kon-Tiki*. The craft, a replica of the rafts used by early coastal natives, reached the Polynesian island of Raroia in 101 days—a distance of 4,300 miles (6,920 kilometers). This established beyond any doubt that early contact could have been made. The lingering question—and a source of major controversy—is whether Old World trans-Pacific contacts may have influenced the rise of culture and civilization in coastal South America.

The Mysterious Nazca

One of the world's great mysteries was etched into the land of southern coastal Peru many centuries ago by the Nazca (or Nasca) people. They, like others inhabiting Peru's coastal zone, had a well-developed tradition of irrigated agriculture. Unlike the Moche, Chimu, and others, however, the Nazca channeled water through a series of subterranean aqueducts (underground tunnels). This practice was widespread in the Middle East but was not found elsewhere in the Americas. Could this be evidence of early trans-Pacific links? Some scientists believe so.

The Nazca are best known for their famous "Nazca Lines." Sometime between 200 B.C. and A.D. 600, they began to use the arid and desolate plains in the vicinity of present-day Nazca as a giant canvas. By the time their work was finished, 300 figures had been had been etched into the desert surface. The features cover an area of nearly 400 square miles (1,040 square kilometers), the world's largest concentration of geoglyphs (earth art). No one really knows why they were created. Suggestions range from the bizarre (an extraterrestrial landing strip) to plausible (religious symbolism, sacred pathways, or a giant astronomical calendar). Features vary from straight lines to very elaborate designs depicting plants, animals, birds, humans, and stylized geometric patterns. What is known is how they were created. Dark surface stones were removed to expose the light colored earth material below. With little rain or wind to erode the features, they have remained one of Earth's most intriguing mysteries for centuries.

The Nazca are best known for the "Nazca Lines," such as this one depicting a monkey. Created between 200 B.C. and A.D. 600, they were originally created by removing darker surface gravel that overlay the lighter-colored subsoil. The dry climate has preserved them through the centuries. No one is sure who "drew" them or why.

THE INCA EMPIRE

By the thirteenth century, Peru had experienced several millennia of cultural growth and development. By any measure, the region was one of the world's most successful and advanced "cultural hearths." It was this cultural setting that gave birth to the Inca, one of the world's most amazing cultures and most highly developed early civilizations. According to legend, one small Andean tribe under the leadership of Manco Capac settled in the Cuzco area around A.D. 1200. Ultimately, this group grew in power to become the Tawantinsuyu (Tahuantinsuyo in Spanish) culture—the name that the Incas gave their empire. It is important to recognize, however, the difference between the (largely

Quechua-speaking) people's culture, which took thousands of years to evolve, and a much shorter period of Inca rule.

Inca society was highly layered. At the top were the Inca—the supreme ruler with absolute authority—and the royal family. Commoners were at the bottom. In between were a number of groups, some more privileged than others but all subject to strict and absolute Inca rule. Every citizen had assigned duties and all citizens also were guaranteed a home and adequate food. The first Inca was crowned in 1438, and the empire fell to Pizarro in 1533. One of the greatest empires in history lasted less than one century.

Once organized, the Inca began to spread their influence rapidly. From Cuzco, its capital, Tawantinsuyu expanded northward to the present-day border between Ecuador and Colombia and southward into central Argentina and Chile. Most of the territorial expansion was peaceful, even though the Inca had a military capability superior to that of their neighbors. Expansion was cultural. Being "Inca" had many advantages, and "conquered" peoples, with few exceptions, were eager to accept Quechua as their language and adopt the Inca social, economic, and political ways of living.

Maintaining control over what was at the time one of the world's most expansive empires was not an easy task. As the Romans had centuries earlier, the Inca added to the existing network of "highways" to link the farthest reaches of the empire to the capital city of Cuzco. Even today, some routes follow the ancient Inca trails. The Inca, though, had no wheeled vehicles. Rather, llamas were the beasts of burden that could carry a pack weighing up to about 80 pounds (36 kilograms). Specially trained runners called *chasquis*, traveling as relays, could transport information and light materials up to 150 miles (240 kilometers) a day.

A very high level of agricultural productivity supported a population estimated at 5 to 6 million in the core region and as high as 37 million throughout the empire. The role of plant and animal domestication and highly successful irrigation in

These terraces of Sacsahuaman were the place of refuge when Incan inhabitants retreated from the nearby city of Cuzco. It is not known when the large stones, some weighing several tons, were put into place.

the region already has been discussed. Other developments included the use of guano as fertilizer, selective plant breeding (improving existing strains), and agricultural terracing. In fact, mountain terraces built for farming cover a greater area of the central Andes than they do in all of Asia!

The Inca excelled at building. Their roadways have been described as being better than those of the Romans. Engineers marvel at their terracing, water diversion and irrigation systems, and suspension bridges. They lacked metal tools, but their stonework was far superior to that of the conquering Spaniards. A thin knife blade cannot be inserted between stones in many of their structures. Sacsahuaman, the huge stone fortress built to protect Cuzco, is said by some military strategists to have been the finest fortress in the world.

The ruins of Machu Picchu are located about 50 miles (80.5 kilometers) northwest of Cuzco. It is believed to have been constructed sometime after A.D. 1400, but the Spaniards never knew it existed. The site was found by American explorer Hiram Bingham in 1911 while he was searching for ruins in the highlands.

Machu Picchu

No Inca ruin is better known or more highly treasured than spectacular Machu Picchu. This magnificent, mysterious, and centuries-abandoned city is located about 50 miles (80.5 kilometers) northwest of Cuzco. Its several hundred stone-constructed buildings are spread over an area of about 5 square miles (13 square kilometers), perched on a mountainside at an elevation of about 8,000 feet (2,440 meters). Almost 2,000 feet (610 meters) below is the narrow valley floor of the rushing Urubamba River. It is believed that Machu Picchu was built sometime after A.D. 1400. No one knows why it was constructed. Most theories suggest that it fulfilled a ceremonial function or perhaps served as a vacation retreat for the Inca.

Even though the site has several hundred structures—including palaces and temples, storage rooms and baths, and numerous houses—and a huge area of terraces, it cannot be seen from the valley floor below. The Spaniards never knew Machu Picchu existed! In 1911, nearly four centuries after the Spanish conquest, an American adventurer, Hiram Bingham, was leading an expedition searching for ruins in Peru. A young boy volunteered (for a dime, as the story has been told) to show the group some ruins. Of his spectacular find, Bingham wrote the following:

> In the variety of its charms and the power of its spell, I know of no place in the world which can compare with it. Not only has it great snow peaks looming above the clouds more than two miles overhead, gigantic precipices of many-colored granite rising sheer for thousands of feet above the foaming, glistening, roaring rapids; it has also, in striking contrast, orchids and tree ferns, the delectable beauty of luxurious vegetation, and the mysterious witchery of the jungle.

SPANISH CONQUEST AND THE CLASH OF CIVILIZATIONS

By the late 1520s, the Inca Empire was divided and distressed. Huayna Capac was the last great Inca emperor, and under his rule, the empire expanded to reach its greatest extent and influence. He drew the Kingdom of Quito (present-day Ecuador) into the Inca realm. On Huayna Capac's death in 1525, the empire was divided between his two sons. The northern realm, centered on Quito, was given to his favorite son, Atahualpa. The rest of the empire was given to Huascar, Atahualpa's half brother and the legitimate heir. A long and costly civil war soon began, pitting the two regions—and sons—against one another. Ultimately, Atahualpa emerged as the victor, but the empire lay in tatters. To make matters even worse, the dreaded disease smallpox had arrived and was beginning to take its toll on the Inca people.

Weakened by civil war and disease, the Inca were on the brink of a third—and, to their civilization, final—shock. The Spanish conqueror Pizarro was on the coast and poised to make his move. Pizarro was the illegitimate son of a Spanish soldier, and according to some sources, he was illiterate and had been a swineherd before joining Spanish forces engaged in New World ventures. With only 3 ships, 180 men, and 27 horses, this Spanish adventurer was planning an almost unbelievable campaign. His small group was about to launch an attack on one of the world's great empires, with an estimated 6 million people and a 30,000-man army!

Pizarro's achievement is amply documented in the historical record. Much of his success can be attributed to the fact that the Indians had never seen a horse and believed that horse and rider were one! Many descriptions are tragic tales of his ruthless, cruel, and unscrupulous treatment of the Inca rulers. In a raging battle, the Spaniards captured the Inca ruler, Atahualpa. A ransom was demanded for his safe return. It was paid in gold and silver worth hundreds of millions of dollars in today's value. Nonetheless, after receiving this vast wealth, Pizarro had Atahualpa executed.

Pizarro's conquest of the Inca Empire was one of the major military feats of history. No military leader had ever conquered as large a territory and none had ever acquired greater wealth for his country using fewer men and resources. Nearly five centuries later, the South American continent continues to be dominantly Spanish in language, religion, customs, and many other aspects of Spanish culture. The demographic (population), cultural, political, and economic aspects of the conquest will be discussed in their appropriate context in later chapters.

This engraving, made in 1595, shows the Inca ruler, Atahualpa, awaiting execution at the hands of Pizarro and his men. In the account written at the time by Pizarro's secretary, Atahualpa was brought into a square, fastened to a pole and strangled, although his ransom had been fully paid in gold.

CONQUEST AND THE CYCLE OF FRUSTRATION

Peru's native culture and history are both a blessing and a source of conflict. Few countries can boast of a grander past, but few also suffer more from the bitter consequences of conquest. The country is divided by race, culture, and history. Europeans hold most power and wealth, whereas the Indian population remains largely powerless and poor. These contrasts contribute to ongoing conflicts that make both political stability and economic development (particularly tourism) difficult to achieve. In the following chapter, you will learn more about the "two Perus" in terms of its divided population and culture.

4

People
and Culture

P eru's estimated 29 million people are sharply divided by both
race and culture. Even their patterns of settlement are divided
geographically: Native peoples dominate the Andean highlands and eastern lowlands, whereas people of Spanish heritage tend
to cling to the narrow coastal plain. A cultural divide is evident in
nearly every aspect of the native and Spanish ways of life, including
language. Only their Catholic faith ties Peru's peoples together, and
even this link is somewhat tenuous. In this chapter, you will learn
about Peru's people and major aspects of their culture.

POPULATION

As is true of many countries, particularly those classed as
less developed, population figures are often little more than
estimates. This is true of Peru. Current figures from generally
reliable sources, for example, list the country's population as being

roughly 27 to 29 million. Most demographic data used in this chapter are based on those found in the *CIA World Fact Book 2004*, "Peru," and the *2003 World Population Data Sheet of the Population Reference Bureau.*

In mid-2004, Peru's population stands at an estimated 28,870,000 and is growing at a rate of about 1.6 percent per year. This figure is slightly above the world average of 1.3 percent, but below the 1.9 percent rate for LDCs (Less Developed Countries). The total fertility rate (average number of children to which a woman gives birth) is 2.81. This figure is identical to the world average and well below the average for LDCs. During the last half of the twentieth century, the country's rate of natural increase (RNI) was explosive. The population more than tripled during the past 50 years. In recent decades, however, the RNI has declined by more than one percent and the downward trend continues. Nonetheless, one-third of the population is younger than 15 years of age, which suggests that the birth rate will remain high for some time.

Life expectancy at birth is slightly more than 70 years. Females outlive males by a margin of 73.5 years to 68.5. The median (average) age of Peruvians is 23.5 years, and only 5 percent of the population is 65 years of age or older.

The concept of "overpopulation" is difficult to define. Some people equate the condition with crowding. Peru's population density is a relatively low 55 people per square mile (35 per square kilometer). This compares with the world figure of 122 per square mile (76 per square kilometer) and the U.S. density of 78 (48 per square kilometer). It must be remembered, however, that more than half the country has a very low population, which creates the low population density. Numbers of people and their density do not suggest that a condition of overpopulation exists in Peru. Widespread poverty and a relatively low standard of living endured by many Peruvians do suggest, however, that some imbalance exists between the country's socioeconomic conditions and its population. Yet about 91 percent of the country's people over age 15 are able to read and write. A highly literate population provides a strong foundation of human resources on which a country's economy can build.

SETTLEMENT

Settlement pertains to where people live, such as sections of a country or region, or urban versus rural place of residence. Today, more than half of all Peruvians live in the coastal region. Another third of the people live in the highlands region, leaving the eastern half of the country to only a handful of residents, perhaps 10 percent of the total population. In the world's LDCs, about 60 percent of the population is rural and 40 percent urban. Peru is an exception in this respect, because 72 percent of all Peruvians live in cities. In fact, nearly one of every four citizens resides in Lima, the country's capital.

Lima is Peru's largest city, with an estimated population of 8.4 million. It is a "primate" city, a city that is the country's population, political, economic, and cultural center. Metropolitan area (city and suburbs; 2004 estimates) populations for other large cities include Arequipa (population 865,000), an industrial city in the southwest; Trujillo (pop. 751,000), Chiclayo (pop. 620,000), Piura (pop. 376,000), and Chimbote (pop. 346,000), all commercial and agricultural centers in the northwest; and Callao (pop. 440,000), the port city for Lima. In the Andes, Huancayo (pop. 366,000) and the ancient Incan capital, Cuzco (pop. 342,000), are the largest urban centers. Cuzco, the old Inca capital, is a tourist center and gateway (by rail) to Machu Picchu. The largest city in the Peruvian Amazon is the river port city of Iquitos (pop. 416,000) whose residents are among the world's most isolated. Iquitos can be reached only by river or air. It has neither highway nor rail links to the outside world.

During recent decades, settlement in Peru has been marked by two major migration trends: rural to urban and highland to lowland. People are fleeing the country for the city in search of

Cuzco's Plaza de Armas is one colonial square in that city that was the capital of the Inca empire and is a thriving city today.

a better life. Urban population growth, however, far exceeds the economic capacity cities have to provide full employment and services for this booming population. The result is the slums, or squatter settlements, that surround most cities. Peru's urban centers are no exception, and the cities continue to grow at an alarming rate.

The second trend has been migration from the highlands to the coast. For nearly three decades (the mid-1960s to the mid-1990s), the highlands were ravaged by one of the world's most ruthless terrorist groups, the Sendero Luminoso ("Shining Path"). Hundreds of thousands of people fled from their Andean homes and moved to coastal cities in the hope of escaping the terrorists' wrath. Many of these migrants were poor, rural, Indian peasants. They lacked the skills (such as literacy and fluency in Spanish) needed to compete economically in an urban environment. This migration contributed substantially to the explosive population growth and resulting social and economic problems that beset Peru's coastal cities.

WHAT IS A "PERUVIAN"?

Peru's people are called Peruvians. They are as varied and diverse as the country's landscapes and climates. People can be classified in many ways. Two of the more common distinctions are race and ethnicity.

Race

Racial lines tend to be quite blurred and of little significance. In Peru, people are judged more on the basis of their culture (way of life) and socioeconomic status. In terms of their racial (biological) inheritance, Peruvians represent all three dominant races: Mongoloid (Amerindians and Asians), Caucasoid (Spaniards and, to a much lesser degree, other Europeans), and Negroid (blacks). Most Peruvians are of mixed ancestry. In fact, the second most common racial element in the population is mestizo, a blend of Spanish/Caucasian and Indian/Mongoloid racial strain. Peru's Indian populations differ greatly in physical appearance, suggesting different origins, including early trans-Pacific linkages. The sharpest differences are evident between Indian groups in the Andean Highlands and those of the Eastern Lowlands, who differ greatly in physical appearance.

Ethnicity

Amerindians (the most acceptable term used to designate the native population) constitute Peru's dominant cultural (ethnic) group, with 45 percent of the population. They are clustered primarily in the highlands and eastern lowlands. Mestizos account for 37 percent of the population. Eighty-two percent of Peru's people, therefore, are all or part Amerindian. In South America, only Bolivia and Ecuador have a higher percentage of the population as Amerindian or mestizo.

Fifteen percent of Peru's people are white, and nearly all of them are of Spanish ancestry. After the conquest in the early 1530s, many Spaniards remained in Peru. There were very few Spanish women, however, at least during the early decades of settlement. Many Spanish men therefore married Amerindian women, which explains the high proportion of mestizos in the country's present-day population. People of European ancestry are found primarily in cities of the coastal plain, particularly Lima.

About 3 percent of the population is black, Japanese, Chinese, or other. Most blacks are descendents of slaves that Spaniards brought to Peru between the seventeenth century and 1854, when slavery was abolished in the country. Because Peru never developed a plantation economy, the number of blacks was small and today amounts to about one percent of the population. Their position on the socioeconomic scale remains low, and most blacks hold menial jobs in the country's urban centers.

The Japanese, too, are few in number, with an estimated 100,000. Most Japanese are well educated and live in cities along the coast, where many are leaders in the business community. One native-born person of Japanese ancestry, Alberto Fujimori, recently served as the country's president.

Another ethnic group, the Chinese, arrived in large numbers, an estimated 100,000, between 1850 and 1875. Some replaced freed slaves as workers on haciendas (large coastal estates). Others mined the rich guano deposits on the coastal islands or worked as laborers on the building of Peru's railroad network. Today, Peru has more Chinese restaurants than any other South American country, more than 2,000 of them. Lima even has a thriving Chinatown!

LANGUAGE

Do you know the language spoken by the greatest number of people in South America? Most people quickly answer "Spanish" to this question. Actually, it is Portuguese. Portuguese-speaking Brazil has roughly half the population of South America. In the central Andes, however, an estimated 12 to 15 million people speak only Amerindian tongues, whereas almost all Brazilians speak Portuguese.

Early peoples in what is now Peru spoke many different languages. During the period of Inca expansion, however, their language—Quechua—spread rapidly and widely. By the time of the Spanish Conquest, most Amerindians in Peru spoke that language. The major exceptions were peoples in the eastern lowlands, an area avoided by the Inca because of the threat of tropical diseases.

Peru's native cultures did not have a written language. Rather, they used what scientists now recognize to have been one of the world's most unique systems for recording information—the *quipu*. Quipus have been described as looking a bit like the working end of a multicolored mop. Information was encoded on a series of cords of different color, ply, and fiber using different types of knots. By these means, the Inca were able to record both numerical and written information. Students of language now believe that the quipu system

Quipus have been the subject of study for many years. William Burns, a retired British textile engineer living in Peru, believes that the multicolored knots are a type of shorthand for the Quechua language.

far surpassed Middle Eastern cuneiform writing, Egyptian hieroglyphics, and other early systems of symbolic writing. Unfortunately, the key to understanding the system is lost.

No one knows how to decipher this brilliant, but now inde-cipherable, system of information storage.

In present-day Peru, both Spanish and Quechua are "official" languages. Spanish is the dominant tongue along the coast, but in the highlands, many people speak only Quechua or, in the area around Lake Titicaca, Aymara. Quechua was the language of the Tawantinsuyu (Inca) Empire, and it is still spoken almost exclusively in the countryside and smaller villages of the highlands. A number of Quechua words have entered English by way of Spanish. Common food-related terms include *jerky* and *potato*. *Condor, guano, llama,* and *puma* are borrowed words that pertain to animal life. Others include the words *coca, gaucho* (Argentine cowboys), *Inca,* and *pampa* (the plains of Argentina). English is spoken by a small number of well-educated Peruvians, many of whom are involved in international activities of some kind.

RELIGION

When traveling in Peru (or elsewhere in Latin America), one cannot help but notice the overwhelming dominance of religion on the cultural landscape. In settlements traced to early cultures, towering pyramids, shrines, and other structures and features attest to the importance of religion. Today, in all but the largest cities, religious structures rise above all other build-ings and otherwise dominate the urban architecture. The huge Monasterio de Santa Catalina, built in 1579 in Arequipa, is not only Peru's largest and most important religious structure, it is also the world's biggest convent.

Peru's preconquest peoples practiced a variety of native faiths. During the Inca era, the Inca religion spread widely through the region. The faith was dominated by three sacred symbols. Worship focused on Inti, the sun god, whose rays gave life and warmth; Pachamama, mother of Earth; and Quilla, the moon and wife of the sun. The Inca believed in the past, present, and future, as do most Christians. Rituals included sacrifices of both humans and animals. At a time of crisis, several hundred children might be sacrificed. The Inca (ruler) claimed to be the son of the sun. Many sacred structures (including possibly Machu Picchu) were built throughout the Inca Empire. After the conquest, Spaniards forbade the practice of the Inca religion. Unfortunately, most Inca religious structures also were destroyed by the Spaniards, whose own religion was soon imprinted on the country's cultural landscape. Among many of Peru's Amerindians, religious practices today represent a blend of the imposed Christian faith and selected practices from native religious traditions.

Spanish conquistadores sought three things in the New World: gold, glory, and God—the spread of their Roman Catholic faith. The Catholic faith, more than any other single trait of Spanish culture, became widespread throughout the region. Today, about 90 percent of Peru's population claims to be Catholic. Only a very small number of people are Protestant or members of some other faith. The largest non-Catholic minority faith is Jehovah's Witnesses, with about 80,000 followers.

Many American and European Catholics are shocked when they see or otherwise learn of some Latin-American Catholic practices. For example, Peru was deeply involved in the Spanish Inquisition. Visitors to the Inquisition Museum in Lima are shocked by the methods of torture that the Inquisition used in punishing heretics. Jews and Protestants were particular targets. Although the Inquisition appeared to be religious in nature on the surface, some historical geographers disagree. It seems likely that suppressing economic (and perhaps political) competition also played a key role. North European colonial and trading powers such as the British and Dutch, were, after all, Protestant, and many Jews also were very successful traders.

The Spanish conquistadors sought the spread of their Roman Catholic faith and in this endeavor they were successful. Today, nearly 90 percent of the Peruvians are Catholic. On October 5, 2002, thousands of pilgrims flocked to Lima to celebrate the day of the "Lord of Miracles," the patron saint of Catholics in Peru.

POPULATION, CULTURE, AND THE CYCLE OF FRUSTRATION

Peru's diverse population, settlement, and culture add to the country's frustrations. Its population continues to grow at a rate well above the world average, and during recent decades, population gain has exceeded economic growth. This condition has further limited the country's ability to provide adequately for its people. Widespread poverty in turn has contributed to political instability. Settlement is uneven. Half of the country, the humid tropical eastern lowlands, has very few people and is poorly developed. Most of the country's population and settlement is in the narrow, dry coastal plain. Lima, in particular, is extremely crowded, and the city is surrounded by urban slum settlements. Such conditions foster poverty, crime, social inequality, and political dissent.

As you have seen, Peru is also divided culturally. The clash of civilizations (and cultures) that began almost five centuries ago continues today. Spaniards continue to be the country's dominant social and economic force. Mestizos follow, trailed by Amerindians who generally remain poor and powerless. If Peru is to prosper, the inequalities existing among its diverse people must be overcome. Until then, the country will continue to suffer a seemingly never-ending cycle of frustration resulting from the diversity of its people, settlement, and culture.

5

Political History and Government

Ⅰn the early morning of June 16, 1987, the author and a group of educators from Alaska were in Miraflores, a suburb of Lima. We were scheduled to leave by bus for the airport at 5:30 in the morning, but one member of the group was late. At 5:34, a brilliant flash lit the sky—first white, then red. In a matter of seconds, we were rocked by the sound of a huge explosion. Moments later, debris began to fall like rain from the sky. The Sendero Luminoso ("Shining Path") terrorists had detonated a car bomb that destroyed an entire city block. Our driver was pale and shaking. He told us that had we departed on schedule, we would have been at ground zero of the explosion—and certainly killed. What an unsettling and eye-opening welcome this was to the turbulent world of Peruvian social and economic conflicts and the political unrest they spawn!

A June 1990 Associated Press release on the Peruvian election cited the following problems that the newly elected president would face: "violent, bankrupt . . . many people, in fact, believe the nation has become ungovernable . . . poor communications with isolated mountain and jungle towns . . . inflation . . . wages have lost 50 percent of their purchasing power in the past two years . . . political violence . . . foreign debt the highest per capita in South America . . . labor and public unrest . . . strikes and protests . . . four of five Peruvians lack regular employment . . . drug trafficking. . . ." Many, if not most, of these problems continue to plague Peruvians and their government.

EARLY SPANISH CONTROL

After the conquest, which began in 1532 and was completed (in a military sense) by 1535, Lima became the focal point of Spanish influence. The city was founded in 1535 at a site on the Río Rímac, a few miles inland from the coast. From here, Spanish influence spread rapidly, both within the area and throughout much of the greater region. Politically, the country became the Viceroyalty of Peru, one of several administrative areas in Spanish-claimed America. In Peru, Spanish settlements clung to the narrow coastal plain. The highlands and steamy eastern lowlands were left largely to native peoples. Only the lure of precious metals and zeal of missionaries in search of converts drew Spaniards into the country's interior.

After forces led by South American liberator José de San Martín crushed Spanish forces in 1821, Peru declared its independence from Spain. Spaniards, however, were reluctant to relinquish their control. It was not until 1826 that full independence finally was won, with the help of Venezuelan General Simón Bolívar. Since gaining independence, Peru has had a very turbulent history.

In the first 40 years after independence, the country had 15 different constitutions and 35 presidents. Leaders often treat the constitution as just a piece of paper, resulting in the rule of man taking precedence over the rule of law. Those in power frequently change the constitution. They do not want to be bound by a document that is inconvenient to their needs or that fails to support their own political agenda. As you will see, the trampling of constitutions is not only in the country's distant past.

RECENT POLITICAL TURMOIL

The years since 1980 have been tumultuous for Peru's government. Issues range from the devastation created by domestic insurgencies led by the Sendero Luminoso ("Shining Path"), a group that followed the teachings of the Chinese Communist leader Mao Tse-Tung and the Cuba-based revolutionary movement called Tupac Amaru to the alleged fraudulent presidential elections. As many as 70,000 people may have been killed during the reign of terror that began in 1980 and lasted well into the 1990s. Bombings, bank robberies, kidnappings, assassinations, and terrorist attacks on Western businesses and government offices occurred almost daily, taking a devastating toll on the country's spirit, stability, and economy.

With his promise to end the reign of terror, Alberto Fujimori, a son of Japanese immigrant parents, was elected president in 1990. During the first two years of his office, the terror continued. By 1992, however, Fujimori was able to gain strong military support. With the military behind his effort, he seized almost dictatorial political power in an effort to stop the Shining Path and Tupac Amaru. He did this by imposing emergency powers that suspended major constitutional provisions. Fujimori dismantled the civilian courts and the government's legislative branch with a promise to go after the terrorists.

Fujimori's efforts to destroy the two terrorist groups ultimately proved to be successful. His methods alarmed many Peruvians, however, because he often relied on brutal police and military operations and secret military courts. Through these efforts, thousands of rebels and terrorists were captured and imprisoned, but human rights activists in particular were critical of Fujimori's techniques. They believed that far too many human rights violations were occurring and claimed

¡LUCHAR POR UN ACUERDO DE PAZ!

In September 1992, the founder of the Shining Path, Abimael Guzmán, was captured and incarcerated at the San Lorenzo Island Naval Base. On June 24, 1998, these members of the guerrilla group issued a statement demanding that the government allow Guzmán to appear in public to refute rumors that he had died while being held in the maximum security prison.

that thousands of innocent people were imprisoned by the hooded judges of the military courts.

Although the Shining Path and Tupac Amaru are no longer the threats that they once were, Peru still has terrorists. As recently as 2002, a few days before a visit from U.S. President George W. Bush, a bomb exploded across the street from the U.S. embassy, killing nine people and injuring many others. As this book goes to press, occasional terrorist acts still are occurring in the country.

Great controversy accompanied the presidential election of 2000. By this time, many viewed Fujimori as being too authoritarian. In the election, he carried only a plurality (the greatest number of votes, but not more than 50 percent), although his party secured a majority in the reconvened Congress. This necessitated a runoff election in which Fujimori supposedly received 51 percent of the vote. The election results were questioned, and his opponent withdrew, claiming that Fujimori had been elected fraudulently. The inauguration was marked with demonstrations, and a number of people were killed or injured during the rioting. Fujimori eventually resigned and fled to Japan. In 2001, Alejandro Toledo became Peru's first Amerindian to be elected president. His election offered a beacon of hope to the country's most oppressed citizens, its native peoples. By 2004, however, his popularity had plummeted to a dismal 7 percent, the lowest rating ever for a Peruvian president. Clearly, frustrations continue in the country's political arena.

Throughout Peru's history, constitutional changes have been rapid and unforeseen, although the country does operate with three branches of government. Peru is a constitutional republic, with its current constitution dating back to the last day of 1993.

THE EXECUTIVE BRANCH

Peru's executive branch of government is headed by the president. The constitution provides for two vice presidents, a policy different from that of almost every other country in the world. The president is elected by a popular vote to a five-year term and must receive a majority of the votes. If no candidate receives a majority vote in the election, a runoff election is held

In 2001, Alejandro Toledo became the first Amerindian to be elected president. His election buoyed the hopes of Peru's many native peoples for a better future, but those hopes have been subsequently disappointed.

to determine the winner. A candidate must be a native-born Peruvian and at least 35 years old; candidates for the offices of first and second vice president must meet the same qualifications. They have the same term of office as the president.

An interesting provision in the constitution makes the first vice president assume the role of president while the president is out of the country. If both the top officials are absent from the country, the second vice president serves as president. There is no limit to the number of five-year terms that the president or vice presidents can serve.

The president is advised by a cabinet. Members of the cabinet are appointed by and may be removed by the president. As in all executive branches, it is the duty of the president to enforce the country's laws. In response to the Fujimori era of authoritarian control, the new constitution is designed to keep the president under the document's provisions.

According to the constitution, the president has many powers, including establishing and appointing the cabinet, representing Peru's government at home and abroad, and guaranteeing domestic tranquility and security. He also directs the government, is responsible for enforcement of the laws, can submit bills to Congress, and appoints or can remove the prime minister. The president has a number of other powers, but the constitution is designed to limit these powers of office.

The prime minister is the authorized spokesperson for the government in the absence of the president. Among other things, this means that the prime minister responds for the government during question times in Congress. This office also coordinates the different ministries in the cabinet and is responsible for approving legislative directives and presidential emergency orders.

THE LEGISLATIVE AND JUDICIAL BRANCHES

Peru has a unicameral, or one-house, legislature called the Congress. There are 120 Congress members and even the two vice presidents may be elected as members of the legislative body. The president is not eligible to serve as a member of Congress at the same time he or she occupies the presidency.

Members of Congress are elected by popular vote to five-year terms, and candidates must be voters who are at least 25 years of age and native born.

The powers of Congress include the ability to pass laws and resolutions, conduct special investigations, ratify treaties, and pass the budget. It even has the power to authorize or not authorize the president's travel out of the country.

Peru's judicial branch is headed by the Supreme Court. The chief justice of the Supreme Court is the head of the body and also the head of the country's judicial branch. Judges are appointed by the National Council of the Magistracy. They serve for life unless they are removed for improper conduct. Justices must be at least 45 years of age and native-born Peruvian citizens. They also must have served as a judge or prosecutor for at least 10 years before appointment to the Supreme Court.

During the 1990s, Peru's judicial branch was not independent of the influence of President Fujimori and the emergency powers he seized to fight the terrorists. Military courts had replaced the civilian courts, and hooded judges, hooded to hide their identity, sentenced thousands of suspected rebels to jail. The lack of fair judicial processes was condemned by many within and outside Peru. The present constitution states that judges are guaranteed independence in an effort to restore viable and fair courts. Lower courts are also used, along with justices of the peace, to decide cases for the first time. The Supreme Court hears primarily cases that are appealed from lower courts and cases that raise constitutional questions.

LOCAL GOVERNMENTS

Local governments are not particularly powerful because, historically, Peru has had strong central government control. Local governments exist, but they are very dependent on the central government as their primary source of funding. There are two main levels of local government, the municipal and the regional levels. Municipal governments were first established in 1963. They had a short life, however, as military rule soon halted this level of government until 1980, when it was reestablished. Municipalities have some ability to tax and charge for licenses, but most of their funding, too, comes from the goodwill of the national government. Taxes generally bring little to the coffers (treasuries) of municipal governments, because the population is poor and few citizens own homes. Lacking adequate funds, municipal governments generally are unable to sustain the basic level of services needed in many areas. This means that roads are often unpaved and electricity and water services may be very limited.

Municipalities were also greatly affected by the terror of the Shining Path in the late 1980s, when hundreds of mayors and other municipal officers were assassinated. The Shining Path targeted these officials in their efforts to increase insecurity. Many other municipal candidates resigned in fear in the months before the 1989 local elections.

The 1979 constitution established regional governments in Peru. Twenty-five regions were created, replacing the departments that previously had provided regional governance. This level of government also suffers from a deficit of funding from the national government, which severely limits its ability to deliver services.

Recent exciting changes have been introduced to decentralize power in Peru. In 2003, President Alejandro Toledo, assisted by international technical advice and funding from the United States and Japan, initiated efforts to move more power to the local levels. The process has had a strong start and is showing promise of giving more political power to local governments. This also may change the local institutions, because more effective local governments could be created to replace the municipal or regional governments that historically have been of limited effectiveness.

CITIZENS' RIGHTS AND RESPONSIBILITIES

The rights and freedoms of citizens have varied greatly during recent decades. Rights, including freedom of expression, were suppressed during the Fujimori presidency as he attempted to end the civil strife created by rebels. Conditions have now eased and individual rights are better safeguarded by the constitution, although problems still exist in the courts and prisons. The country faces the lingering legacy of recent terrorism and a continuing record of human rights violations related to suspected rebels and has initiated a truth and reconciliation procedure that in 2004 is in the process of being fully implemented. Constitutionally, the people are guaranteed a number of freedoms:

- Equality before the law

- Freedom of religion

- Freedom of expression

- Right to privacy

- Freedom of movement and the right to choose where to live

- Right to assemble peacefully

- Right to own property

- Rights to a fair arrest and trial

The constitution assigns some responsibilities to citizens. The responsibilities expressly stated include the responsibility to participate in their municipal government, the duty of honoring Peru and protecting the country's national interests, and the responsibility to respect, obey, and defend the constitution and the country's code of laws.

Midway through the first decade of the twenty-first century, the Shining Path still is somewhat active in Peru. With continuing hostilities, the threat to constitutional rights increases and individual freedom can be repressed or restricted. Rebels know that this is a predictable political outcome of their terrorist activities. They gain power when the government becomes more restrictive, resulting in the increased frustration of citizens. The actual freedoms and rights given by Peru's constitution will remain precarious for some time to come.

FOREIGN RELATIONS

Peru is active on the international stage and has been a member of the United Nations since 1949. Peruvian Javier Perez de Cuellar even served as UN secretary general from 1981 to 1991, a tremendous honor for any nation. The country belongs to the Asia-Pacific Economic Cooperation group (APEC), the World Trade Organization (WTO), and the World Health Organization (WHO). In addition, Peru is active in the Organization of American States (OAS), the International Monetary Fund (IMF), and the United Nations Educational, Scientific and Cultural Organization (UNESCO). The country also plans to become fully integrated into the Andean Community, a free trade association.

Peru also has signed a number of international agreements. These include the Antarctic Treaty and the Nuclear Test Ban Treaty. Other efforts include participation in programs designed to protect the ozone layer, decrease hazardous wastes, regulate whaling, and work to moderate climate change.

Border disputes have plagued Peru for hundreds of years: Contested boundaries with Chile and Ecuador often have led to armed conflict. Both of these disputes seem to have been resolved during recent years. In fact, in 1999, President Fujimori was the first Peruvian leader to visit Chile. Settling these disputes may lead to new trade arrangements and also may develop new contacts between citizens of these countries.

Political stability must be achieved for Peru to be viewed as a dependable trading, investing, and political partner. The internal disputes and rebel efforts pose continuing threats that can destabilize the government and threaten economic development. The nests of poverty in the country serve as rich beds for recruitment of rebel members and for fomenting (inciting) domestic insurrection. Peru's success as a nation will be determined not only by its ability to suppress rebel efforts, but also by its ability to create work and raise the economic livelihood of its poor.

POLITICS AND THE CYCLE OF FRUSTRATION

Politically, Peru also appears to be locked into a continuous cycle of frustration. The country is deeply divided by its physical geography, population distribution, and racial and ethnic makeup of its people. Huge disparities exist in the socioeconomic well-being of its citizens. Inadequate linkages place large areas of the country outside the realm of effective national control. Inadequate revenue makes it difficult, if not impossible, for the government to adequately provide essential services such as health care, education, clean water, and waste disposal. Terrorist groups, the international drug trade, and widespread corruption all contribute to making political stability difficult to attain in Peru.

6

Peru's Economy: Problems and Prospects

A line graph showing Peru's economy over time would look much like a roller coaster—a series of sharp rises followed by rapid descents. Few countries in the world can match Peru's history of economic "boom and bust" cycles. The vast wealth of the Inca was followed by the ruin of conquest. Soon, however, the Spaniards began mining precious ores, taking billions of dollars (in today's currency) of wealth from Earth's storehouse. Since gaining its independence, the country's economic fortunes have been subject to many forces.

In many respects, nature has been kind to Peru—but it can be extremely cruel, as well. El Niño events can cause devastating flooding, destroying roads, railroads, agricultural fields, and even communities. A variety of natural disasters, including earthquakes and avalanches, can have a terrible effect on the country. Mineral resources, on which the country depends for foreign currency, eventually are exhausted. During recent decades, the country has been a world leader in fishing, yet the harvest can dwindle to almost nothing during an El Niño event. These and other natural events can take a severe toll on the country's economy; so, too, do social divisions and unrest, inept and corrupt politicians, government, disruptive terrorism, and many other domestic problems. Economic development is hindered further by inadequate transportation facilities, a lack of capital, frequent inflation, and meager human resources resulting from the general low level of educational attainment. Yet there have been periods during which the country's economy has prospered.

OVERVIEW OF THE ECONOMY

Economic figures for Peru or any other LDC can be misleading. The fact that the average Peruvian has an income roughly equivalent to $4,500 in the United States, or that 50 percent of the country's population lives below the poverty line, suggests tremendous economic hardship. Economic conditions, however, must be considered in the context of the particular culture to which they apply. In Peru, for example, many people continue to live in a traditional culture. Goods are bartered (traded), and human labor is not measured in monetary value. People in a folk culture, such as many of Peru's Amerindians, may work 12 or more hours a day (particularly women), but their labor and contributions do not appear in the country's economic statistics. They may be able to provide all of life's necessities and more and be the envy of their community, yet by the traditional measures used in the Western industrial world, they are "poor." Such differences must be understood when judging a country's economic statistical data.

Peru's economy is unbalanced, with conditions being as diverse as the country's physical geography. A tremendous imbalance exists between the standard of living of the urbanites and the rural peasants. Most economic production, particularly commercial agriculture, manufacturing, and services, is centered in the coastal region. The highlands and eastern lowlands lag far behind in terms of development and the infrastructure on which economic growth depends.

Traditional culture includes the use of a handloom by women to create colorful weavings that can be used or sold as handicrafts to tourists.

Despite these problems, during the early years of the twenty-first century, Peru's economic growth was the strongest in Latin America. The terrorist movements that had plagued the country for more than a decade had abated. Fujimori's strong-handed government was a bad but distant memory. Privatization of industries was occurring at a rapid pace in an increasingly free market economy. Inflation, which has exceeded 10,000 percent in the recent past, was under control. Despite these and other signs of optimism, dark clouds are again gathering over the country's economic landscape. Strikes by government workers, continued political instability, increasing terrorist activity, the growing influence of the drug trade, and increased taxes are among the many factors that have resulted in declining productivity and confidence. Jobs creation is a huge issue in Peru. Approximately 10 percent of the population is unemployed, and 50 percent of the work force is underemployed (they have jobs but are unable to make an adequate living).

Peru's labor force of 7.5 million people is distributed among occupations that include agriculture, mining, construction, manufacturing, transportation, and a variety of services. In terms of contributions to the national economy, services (such as banking, education, medical, legal, transportation, media, and social) account for nearly two-thirds of the nation's gross domestic product (GDP). Manufacturing industries and agriculture trail with a distant 27 percent and 10 percent, respectively, of the GDP.

The following discussion of occupations and industries is organized according to the division most frequently used by geographers and economists. It includes primary, secondary, and tertiary industries as the major categories.

PRIMARY INDUSTRIES

Primary industries exploit natural resources, such as minerals, soil, forests, and the sea. Mining, farming, and fishing have been the mainstays of the Peruvian economy for centuries. These activities sustained the early Amerindian populations and they continue to be important today.

Mining

Peru produces and exports about 30 different minerals and is one of the world's leading producers of lead, zinc, silver, and gold. Minerals have been a major part of Peru's exports and a primary source of foreign currency for nearly four centuries. Early Amerindians, and later the Inca, extracted huge hoards of gold as early as 1000 B.C., and this precious metal and silver were the primary "magnets" that attracted Spaniards to the central Andean region. Gold was the most important ore to the Amerindians and Spaniards, but today, copper, zinc, silver, iron, molybdenum, and tungsten are the primary metals. Other minerals of importance include mercury, uranium, sulfur, and phosphate.

Cerro de Pasco, located in the mountains northeast of Lima, is Peru's chief mining center. At an elevation of 14,000 feet (4,270 meters), the city is one of the world's highest. It is also known as the city that moves itself. As in so many mining communities, parts of Cerro de Pasco periodically must be moved as a huge open pit mine expands in the heart of the city. According to historians, silver was discovered here in 1630 and mining has been the city's chief activity since that time. Silver deposits declined more than a century ago, but the mines still produce other metals, including copper, zinc, lead, and gold. Nearly 80 percent of the world's vanadium (an alloy used in making rust-resistant, high-speed precision tools) comes from the nearby Minasraga mines. Other important mining activity occurs at numerous sites throughout the country, particularly in the south.

Peru has small deposits of petroleum, natural gas, and coal. Still, the country consumes nearly twice as much energy as it produces. Petroleum production occurs primarily in the far northern coastal region, near Talara.

Although Peru is very rich in mineral resources, most of the country's 4,000 mining centers are located in the Andes. This poses several problems. Few places in the world are more difficult to work. Because of the elevation (with less oxygen in the atmosphere), work is very fatiguing. Most miners last only a few years before they are worn out. Lowlanders find it all but impossible to work the mines, so most of the labor is done by Amerindians whose bodies are accustomed to the rarefied atmosphere.

Access is very difficult and costly to construct because of the rugged terrain. Although the railroad connecting Lima and Huancayo was not built specifically for mining, it serves as an example of the difficulties confronted in building transportation routes into the highlands. It is the world's highest standard-gauge railroad, crossing the Andes at an elevation of 15,806 feet

(4,818 meters). The road runs nearly 140 miles (225 kilometers) and includes 65 tunnels, 61 bridges, and 26 switchbacks or zigzags. Because of the high cost of development, the government has given many concessions to foreign interests (more than 90 percent from the United States) to develop the mines. This policy has proven to be shortsighted; the country has lost much of the benefit it could have had if Peruvian companies had exploited the mineral resources.

Agriculture

Many geographers and historians have noted that all early civilizations were based on a productive system of agriculture. Peru is no exception. It was one of the world's great early centers of plant cultivation and animal domestication. Potatoes—of various sizes, colors, and shapes—were the primary crop that fueled (literally, in terms of human energy) the rise of the Inca Empire. The hardy crop could grow at high elevations and under semiarid conditions. Its yield was high and its tubers were very nutritious. Potatoes could be freeze dried (*chuño*), and the processed meal could be stored for up to a decade. On the steep mountainous terrain, much of the early Andean agriculture was terraced and much of it was irrigated. Llamas provided work and wool, and their meat could be dried and preserved as jerky. The domesticated alpaca also provided high-quality wool.

With the conquest, Spanish crops, livestock, and Spanish tastes were introduced. Wheat became an important crop, and sheep, goats, cattle, and horses began to appear on the agricultural landscape. The Spaniards were not interested in farming; they were soldiers of fortune in search of gold and silver. Food was needed, however, to feed the miners, and animals were needed to carry ore from the mines and to provide tallow for candles, and leather for a variety of purposes. After the conquest, the native population declined and much of the agricultural land—and elaborate system of terraces and irrigation systems—

These Inca terraces in the area of Pisac in the Urubamba Valley are evidence of a productive system of agriculture that has allowed people to grow crops at higher elevations for hundreds of years.

fell into disarray. It is probable that less land is agriculturally productive today and less food and fiber is produced than during the height of the Inca Empire.

Today, agriculture accounts for only about 10 percent of Peru's total economic output, and its importance to the overall economy has declined steadily since the 1950s. In 1958, about 60 percent of the country's people were engaged in agricultural work. Today, the figure has dropped to less than 25 percent.

Less than 3 percent of the land area is devoted to crop farming, with another estimated 20 percent devoted to grazing. Domestic crop production is unable to meet the country's food needs, making importation of foodstuffs necessary.

Much of the Andean agriculture remains at the subsistence level—people raise crops and livestock for their own use. Potatoes, wheat, and barley are the chief crops, and herds of llamas and alpacas grazing on ichu grass are an enduring feature of the rural landscape. In the tropical lowlands, most crops, including manioc, sweet potatoes, and many varieties of fruits and vegetables, also are grown for subsistence. Most commercial crops are grown in the oases that dot the coastal plain, particularly along the northern coast. They include coffee, sugar cane, cotton, and rice, all of which are grown commercially, including for export. During recent years, farmers have begun raising some specialty crops for mid-latitude markets. Much of the winter asparagus sold in U.S. stores is grown in Peru, as are many of the very mild onions to reach our markets.

Fishing

For thousands of years, Peruvians have turned to the sea to harvest its abundant resources. Commercially, however, fishing was an insignificant industry in Peru until the middle of the twentieth century. Beginning in the 1950s and peaking in the late 1960s, the country's marine harvest went from negligible to the world's largest. Chimbote, the center of the fishing industry for a time, became the world's major fishing port. Most of the take is in rough fish, such as anchovies, that are processed into fishmeal or fish oil, both of which are exported.

Fishing is a "boom or bust" aspect of the economy. When conditions are normal, the harvest is good and many people prosper. During El Niño conditions, however, the catch can plummet to almost nothing. In 1971 (and on other occasions), a devastating El Niño struck. Its warm waters killed most of the plankton, the primary food of anchovies, sardines, tuna, and other fish species. The annual catch dropped by almost 60 percent in one year. As conditions returned to normal, marine populations grew, but overfishing then began to take its toll. Today, the fishing industry has rebounded. Directly or indirectly, it employs 650,000 people and is the country's second-ranking source of foreign currency. China is the primary market for fishmeal and oil. Canned tuna and sardines are exported to a number of countries including the United States.

Lumber

Almost all of Peru's lumber industry is concentrated in the tropical rain forests of the eastern lowlands. Most tree species in this forest (with up to 450 different tree species per acre, or 180 per hectare) are softwoods. Most, however, are of little commercial value. It is the tropical hardwoods—mahogany, rosewood, Peruvian walnut, and others—that are highly prized. Many of the forests are protected by law, but illegal loggers often invade the lands of tribal peoples in search of harvestable timber. This practice has been a major source of conflict in the region. By some estimates, during recent years, more than 100 people have been killed in confrontations between native people and the outsiders.

SECONDARY AND TERTIARY INDUSTRIES

Secondary industries are those that process primary resources and produce manufactured goods. As an LDC, Peru only recently began to develop this sector of its economy. It accounts for between 25 and 30 percent of the country's GDP. Most manufacturing is basic, producing items such as textiles, clothing, cement, and foodstuffs such as beverages and canned goods. Manufacturing for export is negligible. Peru continues to depend on imports for many manufactured goods, including most of its machinery, transportation equipment, iron and steel, and chemicals.

Two-thirds of the country's manufacturing is concentrated in the greater Lima area. The country's largest steel mill—a huge, smoke-belching environmental polluter—is located in Chimbote. Fish processing and the processing of agricultural goods occur in a number of coastal plain communities.

Several things must happen for Peru to develop industrially. Its infrastructure must be improved, trade barriers must be dropped, its currency (the *neuvo sol,* or "new sun") must be stable, and foreign investment must be encouraged. For these to occur, the government must be reliable, terrorism must be stopped, and corruption must be terminated. Peru is working toward these goals, but is a long way from achieving them.

Tertiary (service) industries are of growing importance in Peru and today contribute nearly two-thirds of the country's entire gross domestic product. They include government positions, teaching, health services, tourism, and other activities that serve the public, but are not directly involved in resource extraction or processing.

THE "SHADOW ECONOMY"

The full extent of the Peruvian drug trade—the "shadow economy"—is unknown. Some observers believe that it is the country's leading industry. Coca, the plant from which cocaine is extracted, has been grown and used for centuries. Highland Amerindians have chewed the coca leaves with lime (the calcium-based solid, not the fruit) since ancient times as a mild stimulant against conditions of the harsh environment. Today, coca leaves are sold openly in village markets. They can be purchased for about a dollar per pound (.5 kilogram). Tourists visiting the highlands are instructed to drink coca tea as protection against *soroche* (a sickness that results from the high elevation and low amount of oxygen in the atmosphere).

Peru is a primary source of coca used in making cocaine, and there are indications that the growing of poppies, the source of heroin, is increasing. Production is centered in

In 2002, farmers can make a better profit growing coca than any other crop. These farmers are clearing away weeds from around the newly planted coca crop in a town called San Francisco. Coca has been grown and used for centuries and today Peruvian coca is used to make cocaine for the illegal drug trade.

the eastern, tropical Andean valleys and slopes. The valley of the Río Huallaga is the major area for growing coca. By one government estimate, at least 125,000 acres (about 50,000 hectares) of land are devoted to the growing of coca. An estimated 200,000 Peruvians profit from raising the crop or some other aspect of the drug trade. At the local level, the problem is simply a matter of economics: Farmers can make a greater profit growing coca than they can with any other crop. The price for coffee, the most obvious substitute crop, has dropped to or below the cost of production. Farmers simply are trying to make a living by meeting the demands of drug users in foreign lands, including the United States.

There are costs in addition to the problems directly associated with the production and consumption of drugs. Ruthless gangs control much of the industry. During recent years, there have been signs of a guerrilla resurgence as federal budget cuts limit policing of the areas of drug activity. Evidence suggests that drug money has supported terrorism in Peru, and drug-related influences have corrupted even the country's highest offices. In a country where law enforcement officers make an average of $40 a month, a $10,000-bribe can cause many crimes to go unseen by officials. The United States gives Peru more than $100 million each year in the form of antidrug aid. Drugs are a major social, economic, political, health, and environmental scourge and, unfortunately, the drug trade will not disappear as long as there is demand.

THE ECONOMIC CYCLE OF FRUSTRATION

All aspects of Peru's geography have an impact on the country's economic condition. The physical conditions create numerous problems of access and for development. Many of the native peoples have not been fully integrated into the country's economy; they remain on the edge, living at subsistence level in a largely self-sufficient folk economy. Until recently, population growth exceeded economic gains, a factor that has contributed to a downward economic spiral. Much of the country supports a very low population and therefore is economically under-developed. An inadequate network of road and rail linkages makes the transportation of goods and people difficult and costly.

As has been proven many times, government and economy are very closely linked. Peru's economy often has suffered because of poor government, and a government short on capital resources has its hands tied in terms of providing adequate public services and developing its economic potential. Living in Peru today can be a very challenging experience!

CHAPTER

7

Living in Peru Today

I
t is impossible to stereotype the way Peruvians live today. Just as
there are many environments and many Peruvians, there are
also widely diverse ways of living throughout the country. At
one level, we can think regionally in terms of "three Perus." First,
there is the desert west. This is home to the greatest number of
Peruvians and most of the country's large urban centers are found
here; some are quite European in influence. Many of the people's
lives differ little from our own. If not for the language, you would
feel as comfortable walking the streets in parts of Lima, or its
affluent (rich in material possessions) suburb of Miraflores, as
you would in many cities in the United States. Second, there is
highland, Andean Peru, home to most of the country's Amerindian
peoples. Here, the ways of living vary from extremely traditional
to fast-paced urban in Cuzco and the larger market towns. Finally,
there is the eastern lowland region. It is home to many scattered

This modern shopping mall can be found in Lima, which is one of the largest urban centers in Peru.

Amerindian tribes whose way of life differs greatly from that of people in the la costa and la sierra. Urban centers are few and widely scattered, and only Iquitos can be truly classified as being a city.

Residents of this region are among the world's most remote and isolated peoples.

At another level—one better understood by most readers—are socioeconomic differences. On one hand, there are the urban elite. They are wealthy, generally well educated, have worldly tastes, and often are well traveled. They are quite sophisticated and differ little from their counterparts in any of the world's affluent societies. At the other extreme are the poor. By and large, they are people with little money, little education, little power, and little hope. They live in meager homes and have few possessions. Few people live between these extremes: Peru still lacks a well-developed middle class. Only in Lima and other cities is a middle class beginning to emerge.

PERSONAL CHARACTERISTICS

Peruvians have endured many hardships during recent decades, but they remain optimistic and strong willed. Most people love their country, are strongly nationalistic, and want both themselves and Peru to succeed. They long for a return to strong and fair democracy. In their relationships with others, they are generally helpful and eager to please. As is true with most peoples, good judgment is needed in discussing such matters as religion, politics, and social issues. Peruvians tend to be polite and respectful and expect the same in return. In Peru, as in most of Latin America, people are regarded as being more important than time. Rarely do things begin on schedule, although this is beginning to change in urban settings, where "time means money" and residents must interact with people from the international business community.

The author has been in all three regions of Peru and has noted great differences in the openness, attitudes, and demeanor of the peoples in each area. Unfortunately, his experience has been limited to several weeks. This is far too short a period of time to develop a valid understanding of chief characteristics and regional differences. One aspect very noticeable from the outset is the sharp division between Peruvians of European descent versus those of Amerindian descent. Similar patterns occur anywhere in the world where European culture has been superimposed on native people and their traditional ways of living. People of Spanish descent are generally urbane (sophisticated), educated, affluent, and in positions of influence. They are fully integrated into what geographers call "popular culture." Native peoples are primarily rural, poorly educated, impoverished, and powerless. Many continue to live a traditional lifestyle, or in what is recognized as "folk culture." These differences are an important source of the ongoing conflicts—including guerrilla movements and terrorism—that have hindered stability and progress in the country.

Personal appearance and clothing—as is true of all other aspects of living—differ on a regional, as well as cultural, basis. Western-style clothing and personal grooming are commonplace in Lima and other urban areas. Rural people, on the other hand, often wear traditional clothing that reflects their individual culture and its traditions. In the highlands, clothing is generally made of hand woven fabrics, particularly wool. One interesting custom is that the style of hat worn by mountain Amerindians indicates the village in which they live. In the rural eastern lowlands, on the other hand, a loincloth may be the only attire worn by remote tribal peoples living in the rain forest.

LIFESTYLE

Lifestyles are as varied as the Peruvian people themselves. Clothing, housing, diet, social relationships, and other aspects of culture practiced by peoples of Peru's three regions differ greatly. Much of the following discussion focuses on practices of the country's urban populations.

Home and Family

Homes in Peru vary from the most modern and expensive structures to humble adobe (mud brick) shelters. In the cities,

Native people are primarily rural and live a traditional lifestyle where family is at the center of life.

the contrasts are particularly striking. Affluent subdivisions contrast sharply with the slums that surround most urban centers. Here, the *norteamericano* (North American) cannot help but notice a major difference in settlement. (Residents of the United States are generally referred to as *yanquis* and *gringos* or *gringas*, neither of which is considered disparaging). In the United States, slums generally occupy the inner city and upscale suburbs dot the urban fringe. In Latin America, residences of the wealthy are clustered near the city center. Slums (*pueblos jovenes*) occupy the city edge and mountainsides. In Lima, there are some exceptions: A few affluent enclaves have begun to appear on the city's fringe.

Families are important to Peruvians. In the past, the average family was large by American standards, but today it typically includes the father and mother and three children. Fathers are the head of family, and, traditionally, women did not work outside the home. They tended to day-to-day home maintenance and child-rearing chores. This is beginning to change, particularly in urban areas, where about 25 percent of contemporary Peru's labor force is female. It is not uncommon for extended families to occupy one home. Newly married couples, for example, often live with the parents, and elderly people may live with and be cared for by their children.

Dining and Food

Peru's culinary history dates back to pre-Inca times and incorporates a wonderful variety of ingredients from its three land regions and the sea. Early Peruvians grew potatoes and maize (corn), as well as squash, beans, and other vegetables and fruits. They also incorporated meat, such as llamas, alpacas, guanacos (a wild ancestor of the llama), birds, and guinea pigs into their diets. Along the coast, fish and other marine life has played a dominant role in the peoples' diets for thousands of years. In the east, Amerindians fished and gathered in the rain forest. They also grew tropical fruits such as avocado, bananas, papayas, and pineapple. Food often is seasoned by aji, a variety of chili pepper.

During the conquest, Spaniards introduced many Old World foods and culinary styles. New animals, including cattle, poultry, and rabbits, were brought in and used as food. Wheat and bread made with flour were introduced, as were many fruits and vegetables. The vegetables included onions, garlic, spinach, lettuce, eggplant, and the important herb cilantro (coriander). Introduced fruits included apples, cherries, and peaches, as well as oranges, lemons, and limes. Rice also was brought by the Spaniards, as was sugar cane to provide sweetening.

Meals in the eastern lowlands are likely to include some type of freshwater fish, starch from a tropical tuber such as manioc or sweet potato, a salad made of heart of palm or another local vegetable, and fruit. In the highlands, guinea pigs, llamas, and potatoes in countless colors, shapes, sizes, and preparations are the primary staples. Along the coast, seafood, rice, and potatoes form the basis of the diet. In the cities, most people eat a light breakfast (*desayuno*) that normally includes fresh bread, jams, fruit juice, and coffee. The main meal of the day (*almuerzo*) is normally eaten at noon. It may include meats or fish and rice or potatoes. Stews are very popular. Street foods (from the carts of the *ambulantes*) are popular, as is fast food and selections from restaurants, including the country's more than 2,000 Chinese eateries. The evening meal (*la cena*) is usually light and can include leftovers, fresh bakery bread, lunch meats, soups, and other light items.

LEISURE TIME

Fútbol (soccer) is the most popular sport in Peru, as it is throughout Latin America. When youngsters are not in school, it seems that every open space, including streets, comes alive with a fútbol match. Teams vary from district and community to school to professional national (assembled for World Cup competition). Other popular sports include volleyball, basketball, and gymnastics.

Recreation in Peru differs little from that in other countries including the United States. No matter what one's recreational interest may be, it can be found somewhere in the country. The author recalls traveling south from Lima and seeing dozens of dune buggies racing around the huge sand dunes that hug the coast.

The Arts

El Condor Pasa may be Peru's best-known contribution to the arts, at least to music. It is a haunting folk song featuring the music of guitar, vertically placed pipes (flutes), and the *quena*— the famous Andean flute, with seven finger holes and a notch to blow against. Today, young Peruvians listen to the music of their favorite rock stars from throughout the world, but people also can enjoy traditional folk music performed by Peruvian artists. Dancing ranges from the most popular contemporary steps to traditional folk dances that are centuries old.

Among Peru's folk arts, Amerindian textiles are particularly well known. Traditional jackets, shawls, shirts, and headwear have grown from simple parts of folk culture to objects of international market appeal. Most familiar, perhaps, is the *chullo* cap with the peaked crown and long earflaps. Everyday clothing may be tailored from llama wool. The fine wool of the alpaca and its relatives, the guanaco and vicuña, are highly prized and rank among the world's most valuable textiles.

Holidays

Peruvians celebrate 11 major holidays, several of which coincide with our own. In chronological order, they include

New Year's Day	January 1
Easter (celebrated Thursday through Sunday)	Date varies
Labor Day	May 1
Countryman's Day	June 24
St. Peter and St. Paul's Day	June 29
Independence Day and National Day	July 28-29
Santa Rosa of Lima Day	August 30
Battle of Angamos Day (Navy Day)	October 8
All Saints' Day	November 1
Immaculate Conception Day	December 8
Christmas Day	December 25

On these holidays, most, if not all, businesses and services are closed. The ways in which the various holidays are celebrated vary with the occasion. Some are religious in nature and quite solemn. Others are times of more festive celebration. Independence Day, for example, is an occasion for bands and fireworks. All holidays tend to be a time for families to gather. Although not necessarily holidays, Sundays are days for families to enjoy picnics, movies, or other entertainment together.

SERVICES

In Peru, public services are limited by the country's inadequate finances. In terms of human development, the country ranks eighty-second among 173 countries according to 2002 United Nations data. Of particular importance in this context, however, is the fact that Peru's rating has shown improvement with each five-year interval ranking since 1975.

Travel and Transportation

Transportation facilities are very unevenly distributed in Peru. Much of the coastal plain is easily accessible by both highway and rail. Most of the eastern half of the country, on the other hand, can be reached only by water or air. The author has traveled by air, rail, bus, and boat in Peru and found that the accommodations vary from state of the art modern (except rail) to primitive. Roads linking urban centers are generally paved, particularly on the coastal plain.

Travel in the highlands is more primitive, with few paved roads. Earthquakes, avalanches, mudflows, and other earth movements can often close mountain roads for days at a time. Some roads and trains reach amazing elevations. One gasps for breath as the train puffs its way over 14,147-foot (4,312-meter) Abra la Raya Pass between Cuzco and Juliaca, near the shores of Lake Titicaca. Even higher is Ticlio Pass: Both highway and railroad reach an elevation of 15,806 feet (4,818 meters) between Lima and Cerro de Pasco, making it the highest pass in the world!

Some trains running through the mountains of Peru can reach amazing elevations—14,000 to 16,000 feet (4,270 to 4,875 meters) at some of the higher mountain passes.

In eastern Peru, ocean-going vessels can ply the Amazon River as far upstream as Iquitos. Here, rivers are the highways and boats—from huge steamers to dugout canoes—are the vehicles of transportation. Each family has its own boat, a necessity for fishing and travel from place to place. On larger streams, some boats are gas stations and others marketplaces. Riverboats also carry people, news, and commodities from urban centers to the most remote villages.

Several national airlines serve most Peruvian cities, and a number of international carriers serve the country's large international airport in Lima. Domestic fares are quite reasonable by U.S. standards. The 1,400-mile (2,250-kilometer) round-trip flight between Lima and Iquitos costs about $120 to $180, depending on date and class. In a country with a per capita income of less than $2,000, however, it can be a very costly trip!

Shopping

Peruvians have one of the world's longest workweeks: It averages 48 hours. Many businesses are open six days a week. As is true throughout most of Latin America, many shops and businesses open early, close for a *siesta* (break or nap) between noon and perhaps 3:00 P.M., and then remain open well into the evening. Shopping varies with location. In villages and even in larger cities, many items—including foodstuffs—are sold in open markets. Visiting an open market is a must for anyone visiting Peru. The sights, smells, people, and activities will linger as one of the most memorable experiences of the trip. In cities (particularly Lima), nearly anything that can be placed on a pushcart is sold by the thousands of ambulantes that wander the streets selling their goods. Today, particularly in larger cities, modern shops and supermarkets (*supermercados*) are becoming increasingly common.

QUALITY OF LIFE

It is difficult, if not impossible, to measure a people's quality of life using standard indices such as per capita income or a country's GDP. Many factors must be taken into consideration, particularly in a developing country such as Peru. Here, large segments of society are in a transitional stage between a traditional, self-sufficient, barter-oriented folk culture and a modern, cash-oriented, popular culture. Their quality of life cannot be measured by the same standards we use to measure ours.

For many Peruvians, having a roof overhead, food on the table, and clothes on their back are all they seek as fulfillment in daily living. Of much greater importance are matters such as safety from terrorists and other criminals, respect in the eyes of their peers, and the hope of a better life for their children. Factors such as these—contributing to peace of mind—can far outweigh material considerations. Many urban people in Peru measure life quality in much the same way as people in the developed world. To them, material possessions, a good job and income, education, annual vacations, and other amenities and comforts tend to be of great importance.

There are a number of different indices of well-being. These surveys generally include factors such as education, employment and income, environmental quality, health and public safety, housing, human rights, and natural security and human safety. One of the most comprehensive surveys is the United Nations Human Development Index. It places Peru at 82 among the 174 countries studied. The most noteworthy of this ranking is, perhaps, that approximately half of the world's countries rank below Peru. This is particularly true considering its recent history of terrorism and political turmoil. Peruvians have a great deal to be thankful for. As the country and its 29 million people look ahead, there are many reasons why they can do so with optimism.

CHAPTER

8

Peru Looks Ahead

"Fascinating," "diverse," "spectacular," and "troubled" are terms and themes that have been used throughout this book. The authors also have emphasized that Peru's problems are closely interwoven, with result that the country and its people seem to be locked into a never-ending cycle of frustration. In this chapter, these themes will be considered once again in terms of the strengths and weaknesses each offers as Peru looks ahead to an uncertain future.

Peru's natural environment and resource base have both strengths and weaknesses. The greatest strength is the tremendous diversity with which nature has endowed the country. No other land has the ocean, a portion of the world's driest desert, a vast tropical rain forest, and glaciers at high elevations—with all of the world's ecosystems occurring (through vertical zonation) someplace between these extremes.

The full potential of Peru's human resources must be harnessed and all Peruvians, including these native children, must be treated equally and come to see themselves as equal citizens of their country.

The country is rich in natural resources, as well, although many mineral resources are in locations that are difficult to reach. The headwaters of the world's greatest river flow eastward, but the desperate need for freshwater lies in the west.

The country's native cultural heritage is rich. Peru was one of the world's great centers of plant and animal domestication. In many respects, native technology was as well developed as any in the world at comparable times. Today, approximately 8 of every 10 Peruvians can trace at least part of his or her ancestry to native roots. With the coming of the Spaniards in the early 1500s, however, there began a clash of civilizations that still reverberates. This clash is very evident in terms of social, economic, political, and even settlement patterns. Peru continues to be a very divided land and people. Until the divisions in opportunity and human well-being are minimized, the country will fall far short of its potential.

Peru's economy places the country squarely among the LDCs. During recent years, however, it has shown remarkable growth. This fact should offer tremendous encouragement, as well as serve as a harsh lesson: Political stability is essential for economic growth. For the economy to continue growing, many things must be accomplished. First and foremost, the relative stability of recent years must continue. Without stability, there will be little incentive for either foreign or domestic investment in the country's future. The infrastructure—highways, railroads, port facilities, power transmission, and communications—must be improved. Of greatest importance, the full potential of Peru's human resources must be harnessed. This means that all groups in Peruvian society must be treated equally. All citizens must have access to quality education, be politically and socially empowered, and be in a position to benefit equally from the fruits of their labors.

In the past, Peru's rate of population increase often surpassed the country's economic growth. This condition has now stabilized. For the country to prosper, its economy must continue to grow at a rate exceeding that of its population. Settlement patterns as they currently exist do not favor development. Only a small fraction of Peru's people live in, and thus assist in the development of, half of the country's territory. The Amazon basin is an area of little settlement and minimal development, but many tropical lands are quite well developed and support huge populations. The key to development in eastern Peru is better access.

Finally, there is the political element of the cycle. As was illustrated in Chapter 5, all other conditions ultimately focus on and affect the country's government. As geographers, the authors have asked themselves, "If I were president of Peru, what steps could I take to bring the country together and make it stronger and better?" Answers to this question do not come easily! Grinding poverty, rampant corruption, a physically divided land, sharp ethnic differences, poor access, and many other problems pose barriers to political stability.

Victor Alba noted that "all of Peru's problems center upon one fundamental problem—the need to convert a country into a nation." A country is a politically governed territory. A nation is a land occupied by a nationality of people, a people who share a common sense of belonging. Many, if not most, Peruvians do not consider themselves "Peruvian." Rather, they identify with their native heritage, ethnicity, or race. For the country to be successful, it must become one nation of peoples. That is, all Peruvians, regardless of ancestry, must pull together for the common good of the country and all its citizens. This will be very difficult to achieve.

To this point, the country's diversity has been considered primarily in the context of the problems that it poses. For a moment, let us consider the many strengths it offers. Lima lies closer to almost any point in the United States than does any European destination, and Americans are the world's most eager tourists. Spectacular physical landscapes, a rich native history, and the Spanish conquest and its aftermath can be a tremendous lure.

Who would not be attracted to a safe and comfortable "jungle camp" along the mighty Amazon or to Amerindian treasures such as Machu Picchu, the Nazca Lines, the ancient Inca capital of Cuzco, or a rural marketplace? Lima is a world-class city in terms of its museums and array of other sites. Ancient mining camps, islands of green oases in the midst of parched desert landscapes, sea birds and guano islands, and towering coastal sand dunes all beckon visitors, as do what may be the world's most remote city of its size, Iquitos; the world's highest railroad; and the beautiful waters of Lake Titicaca. These are just some of the attractions that Peru can draw upon in developing a strong tourist industry. Ultimately, however, the people themselves will be the greatest attraction.

Peru's past has been both glorious and turbulent. Today, the country and its people look ahead to an uncertain future. Most of the country's problems can be solved, though. People of all backgrounds must begin working together to achieve common goals. The government must work for the common good of the people and country rather than for politicians lining their own pockets. Terrorism must cease as a threat to life, property, and potential future investment. Conditions such as these may be difficult to achieve. As Alba noted, Peruvians must begin thinking of themselves as a nation of people. If this goal can be achieved, Peru almost certainly can look ahead to a future as golden as was its distant past.

Facts at a Glance

<table>
<tr><td>Country Name</td><td>Republic of Perú

Conventional: Perú</td></tr>
<tr><td>Capital</td><td>Lima</td></tr>
<tr><td>Location</td><td>Western Andean South America, bordering Pacific Ocean to the west, Ecuador and Colombia to the north, Bolivia and Chile to the south, and Brazil on the east</td></tr>
<tr><td>Area</td><td>496,226 square miles (1,285,220 square kilometers), slightly smaller than Alaska, or combined Texas, New Mexico, and Arizona</td></tr>
<tr><td>Climate</td><td>Varies from humid tropical in the east, to extremely arid desert in the west; wet to dry and temperate to frigid in the Andes</td></tr>
<tr><td>Terrain</td><td>Western narrow coastal plain (costa) with many areas of active sand dunes; high and rugged Andes in center (sierra); eastern lowland plains of the upper Amazon Basin (selva)</td></tr>
<tr><td>Elevation Extremes</td><td>Lowest point: Pacific Ocean, sea level

Highest point: Nevado Huascaran, 22,205 feet (6,768 meters)</td></tr>
<tr><td>Land Use</td><td>Arable land: 2.85%
Land in crops: 0.38%
Other: 96.77%</td></tr>
<tr><td>Irrigated Land</td><td>4,614 square miles (11,950 square kilometers) (2002 estimate)</td></tr>
<tr><td>Natural Hazards</td><td>Earthquakes, landslides, volcanic eruptions, tsunamis, flooding</td></tr>
<tr><td>Environmental Issues</td><td>Deforestation (including illegal logging, particularly in the eastern lowlands); overgrazing in the costa and sierra, resulting in severe soil erosion; desertification; severe air pollution in Lima and Chimbote; pollution of rivers and coastal waters from municipal sewage and industrial/agricultural/mining runoff and wastes</td></tr>
</table>

Physical Geography Notes	Shares shores of Lake Titicaca, the world's highest large lake, at 12,500 feet (3,810 meters), with Bolivia. A remote slope of Nevado Mismi, a 17,441-foot (5,316-meter) peak in southwestern Peru, is the ultimate source of the Amazon River, the world's largest stream in terms of volume
People	Nationality: Peruvians
Population	28,870,000 (July 2004 estimate)
Population Density	58 per square mile (36 per square kilometers); greatest density in coastal plain, very low density in eastern one-half of country
Population Growth Rate	1.6% per year (world average, 1.3%)
Fertility Rate	2.81 children (average number given birth per woman in childbearing years)
Life Expectancy	Male: 68.5 years Female: 73.5 years Average: 71.0 years
Median Age	23.5 years
Literacy	91% (male, 95.2%; female, 86.8%)
Ethnic Groups	Amerindian, 45%; Mestizo (mixed Amerindian and white), 37%; European, 15%; Black, Japanese, Chinese, and other, 3%
Languages	Spanish and Quechua (both official), Aymara and numerous other native tongues spoken by small numbers of tribal peoples
Religions	Roman Catholic, 90%
Type of Government	Constitutional republic
Head of State	President
Independence	28 July 1821 (from Spain)
Administrative Divisions	24 departments (regions) and one constitutional province

Facts at a Glance

Currency	Nuevo sol (3.450 nuevo soles = $1.00 U.S., early 2004)
Gross Domestic Product	Estimated $140 billion (2003, U.S.)
Labor Force	7.5 million
Unemployment	9% (2004 estimate), with up to 50% underemployment
Labor Force by Occupation	Agriculture 25%, manufacturing 9%, services 66%
Industries	Mining, petroleum, fishing, textiles, clothing, food processing, cement, automobile assembly, steel, shipbuilding, metal fabrication, tourism
Agricultural Products	Coffee, cotton, sugarcane, rice, wheat, potatoes, corn, bananas, coca (legal and illegal); poultry, beef, dairy products, wool (sheep, llama, alpaca, vicuña, and guanaco); seafood
Exports	$7.6 billion (2002 estimate)
Export Commodities	Fish and fish products; minerals (gold, copper, zinc, lead), crude petroleum and petroleum products; coffee, sugar, cotton
Export Partners	United States 28%, China 10%, United Kingdom 7%, Switzerland 6%, Japan 6%
Imports	$7.3 billion (2002 estimate)
Import Commodities	Machinery, transport equipment; foodstuffs; petroleum; iron and steel; chemicals and pharmaceuticals
Import Partners	United States 26%, Chile 8%, Spain 5%, Colombia 5%, Brazil 5%, Venezuela 5%, Argentina 4%
External Debt	$30 billion (2004 estimate)
Transportation	Highways: 45,360 miles (72,900 kilometers); 5,800 miles (9,330 kilometers) paved
	Railroads: 1,136 miles (1,829 kilometers)
	Waterways: 5,475 miles (8,600 kilometers), Amazon and tributaries

Ports and harbors: Pacific: Callao, Chimbote, Ilo, Matarani, Paita, Puerto Maldonado, Salaverry, San Martín, Talara; Amazon: Iquitos, Pucallpa, Yurimaguas

Airports: 223; 49 with paved runways; International airport, Lima

International Issues Territorial dispute with Bolivia over the Atacama corridor; major role in the international drug trade; it is a chief source of coca, the source of cocaine, and an emerging opium producer

History at a Glance

B.C.	
c. 20,000	Earliest human presence in what is now Peru.
c. 8500	Earliest evidence of plant domestication.
3000	City of Caral flourishes in Supe Valley.
2000	Many settled villages in coastal zone.
1800	Introduction of corn, improvements in irrigation systems, and beginning of pottery making.
200	Rise of coastal Nazca culture, well known for its formation of various geometrical "lines" in the desert surface.
A.D.	
200–800	Moche culture flourishes.
1000–1470	Chimu Empire exists, with city of Chan Chan as its capital.
1200–1400	Formative period of culture that came to be known as Inca.
1438–1533	Empire and cultural/political expansion from Cuzco northward to southern Colombia and southward to Argentina and Chile.
1532	Arrival of Spanish conquistadores led by Francisco Pizarro.
1533	Spaniards capture Inca capital of Cuzco.
1535	Spaniards found city of Lima.
1542	Pizarro is killed.
1543	Viceroyalty of Peru is created, with its capital at Lima.
1545	Silver is discovered at Cerro Rico.
1570	Inquisition is established in Lima to suppress non-Catholics and economic competition.
1820–1821	General Jose de San Martín's liberation army invades Peru, captures Lima, and proclaims Peru independent from Spain.
1824	Peru becomes the last Spanish colony in Latin America to gain independence.
1849–1874	Estimated 80,000 to 100,000 Chinese people arrive in Peru to perform menial labor such as working on the guano islands, on construction of railroads, and on coastal plantations.

1872	A steamboat begins operation on Lake Titicaca.
1879–1884	Peru and Bolivia are defeated by Chile during the Pacific War, in which Peru loses some southern territory to Chile.
1941	Nearly 7,000 people in Huaraz are killed by flood resulting from glacial ice falling into Lake Palcacocha.
1947	Thor Heyerdahl's *Kon Tiki* voyage proves that navigational contact between Peru and the Pacific islands was possible.
1962	Glacier breaks loose on Nevado Huascaran, killing 4,000 to 7,000 people.
1970	Huge part of Nevado Huascaran breaks loose, cascading into valleys below, killing an estimated 69,000, injuring 140,000, and leaving a half million people homeless; provincial capital of Yungay is destroyed.
1980	Sendero Luminoso ("Shining Path") terrorists unleash guerrilla movement.
1990	Shining Path guerrillas inflict considerable damage on country; an ethnic Japanese man, Alberto Fujimori, is elected president on anticorruption platform.
1991	Fujimori suspends constitution with support of army; Shining Path leader captured, arrested, and sentenced to life in prison.
1995	Fujimori is elected to second term.
2000	President Fujimori resigns amid financial, human rights, and political scandals; he flees to Japan where he remains in exile.
2001	Earthquake (8.4 on the Richter scale) in southern Peru kills 75, injures thousands, and destroys 50,000 buildings; resulting tsunami kills nearly 150 people in Camaná and destroys thousands of buildings.
2002	Alejandro Toledo becomes Peru's first president of Amerindian origin.
2004	Peru faces political crisis as President Toledo's approval rating drops to 7 percent.

Further Reading

Alba, Victor. *Peru*. Boulder, CO: Westview Press, 1977.

Boehm, David A, ed. *Peru in Pictures*. Minneapolis, MN: Lerner Publications Co., 1997.

Dobyns, Henry F., and Paul L. Doughty. *Peru: A Cultural History*. New York: Oxford University Press, 1976.

Gritzner, Charles F. "Third World Peoples and Problems: A Cycle of Frustration," in Gail L. Hobbs (ed.), *The Essence of PLACE: Geography in the K-12 Curriculum*. Los Angeles: California Geography Alliance, Center for Academic Inter-Institutional Programs, UCLA, 1987, pp. 301–313.

Halvorsen, Lisa. *Peru (Letters Home From)*. Woodbridge, CT: Blackbirch Marketing, 2000.

Jenkins, Dilwyn. *The Rough Guide to Peru*. New York: Rough Guides, Penguin Guides, 2000.

Kalman, Bobbie, and Tammy Everts. *Peru: People and Culture*. New York: Crabtree Publications, 2003.

Klaren, Peter F. *Peru: Society and Nationhood in the Andes*. New York: Oxford University Press, 2000.

Landau, Elaine. *Peru*. New York: Children's Press, 2000.

Morrison, Marion. *Peru*. New York: Children's Press, 2000.

———. "Republic of Peru," *CultureGrams*. Provo and Orem, Utah: Brigham Young University and Millennial Star Network, annual editions.

Websites

CIA World Factbook. "Peru" (annual editions). *http://www.cia.gov/cia/publications/factbook*

Geography Home Page. (General information about many topics, including Peru). *www.geography.about.com*

PromPeru. "Peru." Source of general and travel information prepared by the Peruvian government. *www.peruonline.net*

Library of Congress, Federal Research Division, Country Studies. "Peru-A Country Study" (regularly updated). *http://lcweb2.loc.gov/frd/cs/petoc.html*

U.S. Department of State Country Profiles. "Peru." (Annual updates) at *www.state.gov/r/pa/ei/bgn*

Abra la Raya Pass, 94
Aconcagua, Mount, 18
adobe (earth brick) structures, 41,
    89
agriculture, 10, 11, 17, 18, 19, 28,
    36–38, 40, 41, 42, 44–45, 74, 75,
    77, 79–81, 83–85, 91.
    See also drug trade; plant
        domestication
airlines, 96
Alba, Victor, 101
alluvium, 19
alpacas, 25–26, 36, 37, 79, 81, 91
Altiplano, 29
Amazon basin *(la selva)*, 14, 16, 19,
    21, 22, 32, 33, 36, 50, 52, 55, 56,
    60, 63, 75, 81, 86–88, 89, 91–92,
    94, 95–96, 101.
    See also tropical rain forest
Amazon drainage system, 30
Amazon Indians, 33
Amazon River, 10, 16, 19, 28, 30,
    95, 99
ambulantes, 92, 96
Amerindians, 10–11, 12, 13, 16, 18,
    28, 30, 33, 34–38, 40–49, 50,
    54–55, 56–57, 59, 61, 63, 66, 75,
    77, 78, 79, 82, 83, 85, 86–88, 89,
    91, 93, 100
anchovies, 27, 82
Andean Community, 72
Andean highlands *(la sierra),* 13,
    16, 17–19, 20–21, 22–23, 24–26,
    33, 36, 37, 38, 50, 52, 54, 55, 58,
    63, 75, 77–79, 83–84, 86, 89, 92,
    94
Andes Mountains, 9, 10, 11, 14,
    16, 17–19, 22–23, 24–26, 30,
    38, 52
animal domestication, 36, 37, 44,
    79, 100
animal life, 18, 24–28, 32, 36, 91
Antarctic Treaty, 72

Apurimac, 18
Apurimac Canyon, 18
Apurimac River, 30
aqueducts, 40, 42
archaeologists, 35
area, 9
Arequipa, 18, 52, 58
Arequipa-Tacna-Camana area,
    32
arts, 92–93
Asia-Pacific Economic Cooperation
    group (APEC), 72
asparagus, 81
Atacama, 14
Atahualpa, 47–48
Atlantic Ocean, 19, 30
avalanches, 32, 33, 74, 94
Ayacucho, 36
Aymara, 58
Aymara language, 10.
    See also Inca Empire

balsas, 30
barley, 81
barter, 75, 97
basketball, 92
beans, 37, 38, 91
Bering Strait, 35
Beringia, 35
Bingham, Hiram, 47
birds, 18, 24, 26, 27–28, 36, 91
birth rate, 51
blacks, 55
boa constrictor, 27
boats, 30, 95–96
Bolívar, Simón, 63
Bolivia, 8, 13, 16, 18, 55
Bolivian Altiplano, 18
border disputes, 72
borders, 8, 13, 72
Brazil, 13, 56
breakfast *(desayuno),* 92
bromeliads, 26

Index

brush, 25
Bush, George W., 66

cabinet, 68
cacti, 14
Callao, 42, 52
Camana, 32
canals, 40
canyons, 16, 18
capital city. *See* Lima
Caral, 38
Catholicism, 50, 59
Caucasoids, 54
central Andean country, 13
Central Andes Mountains, 24
Cerro de Pasco, 78, 94
Chan Chan, 40–41
charqui (dried jerky), 37
chasquis (runners), 44
Chiclayo, 52
Chile, 13, 14, 72
Chimbote, 16, 52, 81, 83
Chimu Empire, 40–41
China, 64, 82
Chinese, 28, 55, 56, 92
chullo cap, 93
chuño, 79
cilantro (coriander), 91
cities, 10–11, 18, 20, 21, 23, 30,
    32, 33, 38, 40–41, 42, 43, 44,
    45, 46–47, 52–54, 55, 56, 58,
    69–70, 75, 78, 86, 87, 88,
    89–92, 94, 96, 97
    See also Lima
citizens' rights and responsibilities,
    71–72
climate/weather, 10, 11, 19–24, 32
clothing, 89, 93
coal, 78
coastal plain *(la costa),* 16–17, 20,
    21–22, 23–24, 32–33, 36, 37–38,
    42, 50, 52, 54, 58, 60–61, 63, 75,
    81, 86, 92, 94

coastline, 9–10, 14.
    See also coastal plain
coca/cocaine, 11, 83–85
coffee, 81, 84
Colca Canyon, 18
Colombia, 13
communications, 100
Condor Pasa, El, 92–93
condors, 18
Congress, 66, 68–69
conquistadores. See Spanish
    Conquest
constitutional republic, 66
constitutions, 63–64, 66, 68, 69,
    70, 71–72
construction, 77
copper, 77, 78
corruption, 73, 75, 83, 85, 101,
    102
cotton, 37, 38, 41, 81
crime, 61
Cuba, 64
culture, 10, 12, 13, 33, 36, 50–61.
    See also Amerindians
currency *(nuevo sol),* 83
Cuzco (Cusco), 10–11, 18, 20–21,
    23, 43, 44, 45, 52, 86, 94
cycle of frustration, 8, 11, 13, 33,
    34, 49, 54, 60–61, 62–66, 70,
    71–73, 75, 76, 83, 85, 89, 97, 98,
    100, 101

daily life, 86–97
dams, 40
dancing, 93
deer, 36
deserts, 8, 9, 13, 14, 19, 20, 21, 23,
    24, 32, 42, 98.
    See also coastal plain
diet, 10, 37, 38, 40, 79, 81, 91–92
dinner *(almuerzo),* 92
diseases, 10, 32, 48, 56, 83
drug trade, 11, 73, 76, 83–85

early civilizations, 38, 40–42, 58–59
early settlers, 35–36
earthquakes, 10, 17, 30, 32, 33, 74, 94
Easter Island, 41
economic cycle of frustration, 85
economy, 11, 13, 19, 33, 49, 60, 73, 74–85, 100–101
Ecuador, 13, 23, 47, 55, 72
education, 51–52, 58, 75, 83, 100
eel, 27
El Niño events, 10, 20, 21–22, 23, 28, 32, 33, 40, 74, 75, 81–82
elections, 64, 66–67, 69, 70
electricity, 70
employment, 73, 76–77
energy resources, 78, 100
English language, 58
erosion, 19
ethnicity, 55–56
Europeans, 86, 89.
    See also Spain; *under* Spanish
evening meal *(la cena)*, 92
executive branch, 66–68.
    See also presidents
exports, 77, 81, 82

families, 91, 94
fast food, 92
ferns, 24
fertility rate, 51
fertilizer, 28, 41, 45, 56
fishing, 75, 81–82, 91, 96.
    See also marine resources
flooding, 10, 20, 22, 32–33, 40, 74, 75, 81–82
flowering plants, 24
fog *(garuá/garrua)*, 23–24
fog zone *(loma)*, 24
folk culture, 89, 92–93.
    See also Amerindians; Inca Empire
folk economy, 75, 85, 97

food. *See* diet
foreign currency, 74, 77, 82
foreign investment, 79, 83, 100
foreign relations, 72–73
free market economy, 76
fruits, 91, 92
Fujimori, Alberto, 56, 64–66, 68, 69, 71, 72, 76
fútbol (soccer), 92
future, 8, 97, 98–102

geoglyphs (earth art), 9, 42
glaciers, 9, 18, 19, 21, 33, 35, 98
goats, 79
gold, 77, 78, 79
government, 13, 33, 56, 62–63, 66–73, 75, 76, 83, 85, 88, 101, 102.
    See also political history/ frustration
grasslands *(puna)*, 14, 25–26, 36
gringos/gringas, 90
gross domestic product (GDP), 77, 82
guanaco, 36, 91, 93
guano, 27–28, 41, 45, 56
guinea pigs, 91, 92
gymnastics, 92

haciendas, 56
hats, 89, 93
health care, 10, 56, 83
heroin, 83–84
Heyerdahl, Thor, 41–42
history, 8, 10–11, 28, 58.
    See also Amerindians; Inca Empire; Spanish Conquest
Hohokam, 41
holidays, 93–94
horses, 48, 79
housing, 41, 53–54, 61, 89, 89–90
Huaca del Sol (Pyramid of the Sun), 40

Index

Huallaga, Río, 84
Huancayo, 52, 78
Huaraz, 33
Huascar, 47–48
Huayna Capac, 47
human rights violations, 71–72
Humboldt, Alexander von, 24
hunting and gathering peoples, 35–36

Ice Age, 35
ichu grass, 25–26, 81
imports, 82
Inca Empire, 10–11, 16, 33, 34, 43–48, 52, 56–59, 74, 77, 79, 80
independence, 63
Independence Day, 94
Indians. *See* Amerindians; Inca Empire
industries, 75, 76, 77, 77–83, 94–96
inflation, 75, 76
infrastructure, 13, 17, 19, 30, 33, 40, 41, 44, 45, 52, 56, 70, 74, 75, 77, 78–79, 83, 85, 94–96, 100
insects, 24, 26, 32
international agreements, 72
International Monetary Fund (IMF), 72
Inti, 58
Iquitos, 21, 22, 30, 52, 87, 95, 96
Ireland, 37
"Irish" (white) potatoes, 10, 79, 81, 91, 92
iron, 77
irrigation, 36, 38, 40, 41, 42, 44–45, 79
islands, 16, 27–28, 56

Japan, 70
Japanese, 55–56, 64
Jehovah's Witnesses, 59
jerky, 79

Judaism, 59
judicial branch, 64, 69
Juliaca, 94

Kon-Tiki, 42

labor force, 77
lakes, 8, 18, 28–30, 33, 58
land features, 16–19
landslides, 10, 20, 32, 33, 94
languages, 12, 13–14, 33, 37, 50, 56–58, 86
Latin America, 12, 34
lead, 77, 78
legislative branch, 64, 66, 68–69
leisure time, 92, 94
leopards, 26
less-developed countries (LDCs), 13
lichens, 26
life expectancy, 51
lifestyles, 89–92
Lima, 10–11, 20, 21, 23, 52, 55, 56, 59, 61, 62, 63, 78, 83, 86, 89, 90, 94, 96, 101, 102
livestock, 10, 25–26, 36, 37, 41, 44, 79, 81, 91, 92, 93
See also animal domestication
llamas, 10, 25–26, 36, 37, 41, 44, 79, 81, 91, 92, 93
local governments, 69–70, 71
location, 11–13
lower class, 88
lumber industry, 82

Machu Picchu, 9, 46–47, 52, 59
McIntyre, Lake, 16
maize (corn), 37, 91
Manco Capac, 43
manioc, 81, 92
manufacturing, 75, 77, 82–83
Mao Tse-Tung, 64
Marañón, 30

marine life, 24, 27–28, 29, 32, 36, 37–38, 40, 41, 75, 81–82, 91, 92, 96
markets, 96
mercury, 78
mestizos, 54, 55, 61
middle class, 88
migration, 52–54
Minasraga mines, 78
mining/mineral resources, 63, 74, 74–75, 77–79, 99
Miraflores, 62, 86
Misit, El, 18
missionaries, 63
Moche (Mochica), 40
Moche River, 40
molybdenum, 77
Monasterio de Santa Catalina, 58
Mongoloids, 35, 54
monkeys, 26
montaña, 19, 24
mosses, 26
mountain forest, 25
mountains, 8, 9, 10, 11, 14, 16, 17–19, 20–21, 22–23, 24, 24–26, 30, 33, 52.
    See also Andean highlands
municipal governments, 69–70, 71
music, 92–93

National Council of the Magistracy, 69
native cultures. See Amerindians; Inca Empire
natural environment, 8, 9–10, 13, 14, 16–30, 32–33, 98
natural gas, 78
natural hazards, 10, 13, 17, 18, 20, 22, 30, 32–33, 40, 74, 75, 81–82, 94
natural resources, 63, 74–75, 77–83, 98–99
    See also animal life; marine life; plant life

Nazca, 42
Nazca Lines, 9, 42
Nazca (Nasca), 42
Nazca Plate, 17
Negroids, 54
Nevado Huascaran, 17–18
Nuclear Test Ban Treaty, 72

oases, 17, 81
onions, 81
Organization of American States (OAS), 72

Pachamama, 58
Pacific Ocean, 10, 16, 17, 19, 21, 23, 28, 98
Pacific Rim, 13, 28
Palcacocha, Lake, 33
people, 11, 28, 33, 50–61, 88–89, 101, 102.
    See also Amerindians
peppers, 37
per capita income, 75, 96
Perez de Cuellar, Javier, 72
Peru Current, 20, 21, 23, 27, 28
Peruvian Desert, 14
Peruvians, 54–56, 101
petroleum, 78
phosphate, 78
piranha, 27, 32
Pizarro, Francisco, 10, 44, 48
plankton, 27, 82
plant domestication, 10, 37, 44, 79, 100.
See also agriculture
plant life, 14, 24–28, 36
political history/frustration, 11, 13, 34, 49, 54, 60, 61, 62–66, 70, 71–73, 75, 76, 83, 85, 89, 97, 100, 101
poppies, 83–84
popular culture, 89, 97
population, 11, 13, 50, 50–52, 85, 97

population density, 51
population growth, 51, 60, 85, 100
ports, 16, 30, 42, 52, 81, 100
Portuguese, 56
potatoes. *See* "Irish" white potatoes
poverty, 11, 51, 53–54, 60, 61, 70, 73, 75, 85, 88
power transmission, 100
precipitation, 9, 10, 14, 20, 21–23, 25, 28, 32, 33, 40, 74, 75, 81–82
presidents, 56, 62–63, 64–68, 69, 70, 71, 72, 76, 101
primary industries, 77–83
primate city, 52
prime minister, 68
privatization, 76
Protestantism, 59
puna, 36
pyramids, 38, 40, 41, 58

quality of life, 51, 75, 96–97
Quechua language, 10, 33, 37, 43–44, 56, 58.
    See also Inca Empire
quena (flute), 92–93
Quilla, 58
quipu, 56–58
Quito, Kingdom of, 47

race, 54–55
railroads, 56, 74, 78–79, 85, 94, 100
rainfall, 10, 20, 21–22, 23, 28, 32, 33, 40, 74, 75, 81–82
Raroia, 42
rate of natural increase (RNI), 51
regional governments, 70
religion, 12, 38, 41, 50, 58–59, 63
restaurants, 92
rice, 81, 91, 92
Rímac, Río, 63
rivers, 10, 16, 19, 29, 30, 40, 46, 52, 63, 95, 99

roads, 16, 30, 45, 70, 74, 85, 94, 100
rodents, 26
rural people. *See* Amerindians

Sacsahuaman, 45
San Martín, José de, 63
sand dunes, 17, 92
sardines, 82
scrub, 14, 25
secondary industries, 75, 77, 82–83
Sendero Luminoso ("Shining Path"), 54, 62, 64–65, 70, 71–73, 75, 76, 83, 85, 89, 97, 102
services, 75, 77, 83, 94–96
settlement patterns, 13, 16, 17, 33, 50, 52–54, 55–56, 60–61, 86, 100–101
shadow economy. *See* drug trade
sheep, 79
shopping, 96
shrubs, 25
siesta (break or nap), 96
silver, 77, 78, 79
slaves, 55
slums *(pueblos jovenes),* 53–54, 61, 90
smallpox, 48
snakes, 26, 32
snow, 9, 14, 21, 23, 25
snow line, 21
social frustration, 11, 13, 34, 49, 61, 73, 100
soil, 19
soroche, 83
South American continental divide, 18–19
South American Plate, 17
Spain, 10–11, 12, 13, 33, 37, 44
Spaniards, 11, 16, 28, 34, 37, 47, 50, 55, 61, 63, 89
Spanish Conquest, 10, 44, 47–49, 55, 56, 59, 63, 74, 77, 79, 91, 100

Spanish Inquisition, 59
Spanish language, 58
sports, 92
squash, 37, 38, 91
stews, 92
streams, 16–17, 18–19, 30, 38, 96
street foods, 92
strikes, 76
sugar cane, 81
sulfur, 78
Supe Valley, 38
supermarkets (supermercados), 96
Supreme Court, 69
sweet potatos (cumar), 37, 38, 41, 81, 92

Talara, 78
Talara peninsula, 11
tapir, 26
Tawantinsuyu (Tahuantinsuyo) culture, 43, 44, 58. See also Inca Empire
taxes, 70, 76
tectonic plates, 17, 32
temperatures, 20–21
terrorism, 11, 54, 62, 64–66, 69, 70, 71–73, 75, 76, 83, 85, 89, 97, 102
tertiary industries, 75, 77, 83, 94–96
textiles, 93
Ticlio Pass, 94
Titicaca, Lake, 8, 16, 18, 28–30, 58, 94
Toledo, Alejandro, 66, 70
totora (cattail) reeds, 30
tourism, 8–9, 18, 28, 49, 52, 83, 100–102
trade, 13, 38, 40, 41, 72, 77, 81, 82, 83
transportation, 17, 19, 30, 33, 40, 41, 44, 45, 52, 56, 70, 74, 75, 77, 78–79, 83, 85, 94–96
trees. See tropical rain forest

tropical rain forest (la selva), 8, 9, 13, 14, 16, 19, 21, 22, 24, 25, 26–27, 82, 89, 98
Trujillo, 40, 52
tsunamis (tidal waves), 10, 32–33
tubers, 10, 37, 38, 41, 79, 81, 91–92
Tumbes, 20
tuna, 82
tungsten, 77
Tupac Amaru, 64–65

Ucayali River, 30
underemployment, 77
unemployment, 76–77
United Nations, 72
United Nations Education, Scientific and Cultural Organization (UNESCO), 72
United Nations Human Development Index, 97
United States, 70, 79, 81, 82, 85, 90
upper class, 88
uranium, 78
Uru Indians, 30
Urubamba River, 30, 46

valleys, 19
vanadium, 78
vegetables, 91, 92
vertical zonation, 24, 98
vice president, 66, 67–68
Viceroyalty of Peru, 63
vicuñas, 25–26, 36, 37, 93
vines, 26
volcanoes, 10, 17, 18
volleyball, 92

water features, 8, 9–10, 14, 16–17, 18–19, 21, 27–30, 33, 38, 40, 41, 46, 58, 63, 81–82, 95–96, 99
water services, 70
weirs, 40
wheat, 79, 81, 91

Index

windows to the world, 28.
  See also Amazon River; Pacific
    Ocean; Titicaca, Lake
winds, 20
woodlands, 14
wool, 93
workweeks, 96
World Health Organization (WHO),
  72

World Heritage Sites, 9
World Trade Organization (WTO),
  72

yanquis, 90
Yungay, 32

zinc, 77, 78

Picture Credits

About the Contributors

CHARLES F. "FRITZ" GRITZNER and **YVONNE L. GRITZNER** are both geographers who love Peru. Fritz is Distinguished Professor of Geography at South Dakota State University in Brookings. He is now in his fifth decade of college teaching, research, and writing. During his career, he has taught nearly 70 different courses, spanning the fields of physical, cultural, and regional geography. In addition to teaching, he enjoys writing, working with teachers, and sharing his love of geography with students. As consulting editor for the Chelsea House MODERN WORLD NATIONS series, he has a wonderful opportunity to combine each of these "hobbies." Fritz has served as both president and executive director of the National Council for Geographic Education and has received the Council's highest honor, the George J. Miller Award for Distinguished Service.

The authors have traveled in some 50 countries and regard Peru as being their favorite in terms of its spectacular physical landscapes, historical interest, and diversity. Fritz has visited the country on two occasions, and has visited locations in *la costa, la sierra,* and *la selva.* His wife, Yvonne, now a homemaker, lived in Peru for six years and has many fond memories of her experiences there.